IMPROVE YOUR ENGLISH

Improve your English

Rosalind Birley

Hugos's Language Books Ltd, London

Set in 10/12 Plantin by
Typesetters Ltd
Printed and bound in Great Britain by
Hollen Street Press Ltd

Contents

Preface

This book aims to help you to improve your written and spoken English. Written and spoken English need not be separate languages, as they are often considered to be – one a formula with very fixed conventions, the other a game where every player makes up his own rules. The best conversation is lively, expressive and grammatically acceptable and the best writing is the same.

The most helpful way to use this book is not to read it from cover to cover, but to refer to the sections that interest or concern you most. If you are more interested in improving your spoken English, then **Redundant words and phrases** and **Pronunciation** will be more helpful to you than **Hyphens** or **Punctuation**, which will be useful if you want to write more effective English. Many sections, like **Bad habits** and **Words of similar form but different meaning**, are relevant to both speech and writing. **Grammatical terms** will explain any technical words you may not understand.

You will be a more interesting person if you speak and write clearly, even if you split infinitives sometimes, than someone who never splits an infinitive but seems at the mercy of catch phrases and long-windedness. Indifference to language is often the mark of indifference to sincerity and clarity. The more trouble you take over the precision of the words you use, the more trouble you take to mean what you say.

At the end of the book there are several extracts from various authorities on the use – and misuse – of English. They are intended to raise some interesting questions about the way we use language, and provide some variety to the practical emphasis of other sections. You may like to turn to them before bracing yourself for the complexities of English idiom and grammar.

Bad habits

It is all too tempting not to think about the way you use words. Time is always against you: you have only ten minutes to write a letter; you must make that point before a colleague butts in; you must tell that funny story before the conversation moves on. No, it takes too long and, anyway, isn't it more important to concentrate on <u>what</u> is being said rather than <u>how</u> it is being said? So what, if I tend to repeat myself, if I talk about a crisis situation rather than a crisis and say alibi instead of excuse? Everyone knows what I mean!

To consider that how you speak and write does not affect what you speak and write is naive, and it is downright conceit to suppose that the way words are used bears no relation to character. Slovenly English tends to be the mark of a slovenly person, someone who does not care whether he is using vague words in place of precise words or whether he is blurring valuable distinctions in meaning. The clearer the English, the more lucid the mind using it. An intelligent user of English expresses himself with clarity and precision.

The following list includes the most common bad habits in English usage, with a preferred alternative to each. It should not be difficult to find these examples in the newspapers, on television, in the conversation of others – and on your own lips.

absolute

BAD: It was an *absolute* disaster.
GOOD: It was a (terrible) disaster.

You cannot qualify certain nouns, like disaster or perfection, in terms of quantity. There is no such thing as a minor disaster; similarly there is no such thing as an *absolute* disaster, although there may be a terrible or fatal disaster. *Absolute* is being used to intensify *disaster* – the English are very fond of using intensifying adjectives and adverbs – but the noun already carries sufficient intensity. To saturate it with more weakens the word. You will often hear this done – and catch yourself doing it – in informal English, but try to use *absolute* at its most absolute: *When he said he loved her, he told her the absolute truth.*

absolutely

BAD: 'Do you agree?' 'Oh, *absolutely!*'
GOOD: 'Do you agree?' 'Yes!'

Do not embroider total agreement with clumsy qualification. The brief but effective rejoinder 'Yes' can, if fervently uttered, express all the appropriate enthusiasm. Use *absolutely* only where it is absolutely necessary.

aggravate

BAD: You are *aggravating* her.
GOOD: You are irritating her.

To aggravate means *to make worse*. It has a common colloquial sense, *to irritate* or *exasperate*. Do not use this in formal writing – you will only aggravate the decline of a useful word!

alibi

BAD: Did you pretend to be ill yesterday? What was your *alibi?*
GOOD: Did you pretend to be ill yesterday? What was your excuse?

An *alibi* is a plea that when an alleged act took place, one was elsewhere. The meaning of *alibi* is more specific than that of *excuse*, so the two cannot be synonymous.

all of: see chapter on American English.

all ready/already; all right; all together/altogether

These words are often confused. Note their different usages carefully:

We were *all ready* in the afternoon.
I had *already* written to my M.P.

Do you feel *all right* now?

(NEVER *alright;* but see section on American English.)

We were *all together*, the whole family, that day.
They kept six cats *altogether* in the house.

alternative

WRONG: There is, however, a third *alternative*.
RIGHT: There is, however, a third choice/course/plan/option.

Strictly speaking, there cannot be several alternatives, but two only.

Do not use *alternative* when there are more than two options; there are plenty of better words. *Alternative* is often used as an adjective instead of 'new', 'other'; avoid this unless there is an element of choice implied.

analogous

BAD: This case is *analogous* to the other one; the symptoms are identical.
GOOD: This case is the same as the other one; the symptoms are identical.

Analogous is not a synonym for *similar* or *the same*. It means that something is similar in certain respects, so you cannot use the word in the same breath as *identical*.

anodyne

BAD: The music in the hotel lounge was soft and *anodyne*.
GOOD: The music in the hotel lounge was soft and nondescript.

An *anodyne* relieves pain, whereas the banality of most music in public places is more likely to cause it!

anymore/anytime

WRONG: I don't want to see you *anymore*./Come and see me *anytime*.
RIGHT: I don't want to see you any more./Come and see me any time.

These spellings are American English. British English writes them as two words.

arguably

BAD: He is *arguably* the finest athlete of his generation.
GOOD: I would claim that he is the finest athlete of his generation.

Arguably is arguably one of the feeblest words in the language. It is often used as verbal self-protection, by those who lack the courage of their convictions, and serves no useful purpose.

as of

BAD: This office will *as of* now be closed for lunch every day.
GOOD: This office will from now on be closed for lunch every day.

As of is frequently heard used together with *now* or some other expression of time (*as of today*, *as of next week*), when *from* is the correct word.

as such

HIDEOUS: Do you like classical music *as such?*
ACCEPTABLE: Do you like classical music?

As such is one of those trivializing phrases which have such a destructive effect on the language. Its intentions are deliberately and injuriously vague, always making the object described 'as such' imprecise. Everyone knows what classical music is; but very few can know what classical music 'as such' is.

as to

BAD: I am debating *as to* what I should do next.
GOOD: I am debating what I should do next.

As to is quite unnecessary here. Beware of *as to* with *why, how,* and *where* as well.

attention

WRONG: Mr Headstone has called *it to my attention.*
RIGHT: Mr Headstone has called my attention to it.

Avoid this illogical reversal of the idiom.

basically

BAD: *Basically,* I am in favour of it.
GOOD: Yes, I am in favour of it (, but ...)

Basically, *basically* is one of those overused adverbs with no good, clear meaning. It is a common qualification for those who are afraid to express their real likes and dislikes (*basically* is often followed by *but,* which precedes a real opinion), or for those who think that *basically* adds an extra touch of importance, as in *'Basically, I like it.'*

beg the question

WRONG: I will query that report because it *begs so many questions.*
RIGHT: I will query that report because it leaves so many questions unanswered.

Begging the question means assuming the truth of something which has not yet been proved. It does not mean 'to invite the obvious question (that)' or 'to avoid giving a straight answer to'.

between each/every

BAD: The amount was divided *between each* member.
GOOD: The amount was divided between (all) the members/among the members.

It is best to avoid following *between* with *each* or *every.*

between ... or

WRONG: You must choose *between* him *or* me.
RIGHT: You must choose between him and me./You must choose him or me.

Between should be followed by *or* only in informal writing.

bland

BAD: The lunch and conversation were as *bland* and uninteresting as each other.
GOOD: The lunch and conversation were as dull and uninteresting as each other.

The true meaning of *bland* is not pejorative, although it is becoming so. It is not a synonym for 'insipid'. It means *gentle, smooth, mild, not stimulating.* A cheese may be bland and also good.

can

BAD: Can I come in?
GOOD: May I come in?

This means literally *Am I able to come in?*, which for most people is superfluous. The much-neglected *may* (*Am I allowed?*) is more precise, and more polite in careful English.

charismatic

BAD: He stared at her with *charismatic* blue eyes.
GOOD: He stared at her with compelling blue eyes.

Do not dilute *charismatic* by using it to describe purely physical attributes. Political leaders and great stars are charismatic when millions of people follow or admire them without being able to say exactly why.

chronic

BAD: Isn't the weather *chronic?*
GOOD: Isn't the weather appalling?

Do not use *chronic* to mean 'bad', 'severe' or 'objectionable'. This mistake is so long-standing that it can truly be described as chronic – of long duration.

complex

BAD: This is a *complex* problem.
GOOD: This is a complicated problem.

As an adjective, *complex* is frequently misused for 'complicated'. It has a specific meaning, to describe something which is made up of many parts, and does not carry the sense of being problematic, as 'complicated' does. English may be a complex language, but it is simple to avoid this particular error.

comprise

BAD: The school *is comprised of* five hundred children.
GOOD: The school consists of/comprises five hundred children.

Comprise is never followed by the preposition *of.*

content oneself

BAD: I had to *content myself by* writing an angry letter to the hotel manager.
GOOD: I had to content myself with writing an angry letter to the hotel manager.

Content (one)self is always followed by *with*, not *by.*

continue

BAD: He *continued to remain* obstinate.
GOOD: He continued to be obstinate./He remained obstinate.

This is a tautology, for *continue* and *remain* have the same meaning here.

different

BAD: *Several different* officials attended the dinner.
GOOD: Several officials attended the dinner.

Different is quite superfluous here; *several* by itself indicates the number of officials attending, and, as they clearly could not be identical people, what is the point of stating that they were different?

different than

BAD: It's *different than* what I thought.
GOOD: It's different from what I thought.

Different than is an established American Engish idiom and should generally be avoided.

different to

BAD: It was a *different* outcome *to* what I had intended.
GOOD: It was a different outcome from what I had intended.

Different to is common in informal usage, but *different from* is preferable.

dilemma

BAD: This patient's treatment will be a *dilemma*.
GOOD: This patient's treatment will be a problem.

Dilemma is not a synonym for 'problem'. It means (1) a choice between two or sometimes more than two awkward possibilities or, more loosely, (2) a perplexing situation in which a choice has to be made. Faced with the dilemma of whether or not to use it, think carefully.

disinterested

BAD: The editor was *disinterested* in my article.
GOOD: The editor was uninterested in my article.

Disinterested means *impartial, unbiased;* using it to mean 'uninterested' is very common now. Avoid this wrong use; if you ignore the difference, perhaps you are 'disinterested' in improving your English!

due to

BAD: *Due to* bankruptcy, I must live abroad.
GOOD: Owing to/Because of bankruptcy, I must live abroad.

Due to meaning 'owing to' is unacceptable and avoidable. *Due* can refer to something that ought to have been given (for example, *The rent is due*) or it can mean *to be ascribed to* (*Illiteracy is due to bad education*). In both cases *due* serves as an adjective depending on the verb *to be,* which it does not when it comes to mean *owing to.*

effectively

BAD: *Effectively,* he was criticizing company policy.
GOOD: In effect, he was criticizing company policy.

Effectively is often used wrongly for 'in effect', which itself is rarely a useful phrase. *Effectively* comes from *effective,* meaning having power to effect, being successful in producing an effect: *The threat was effective, for the bill was paid.*

either (of the three)

BAD: *Either* of the three will do.
GOOD: Any of the three will do.

Do not use *either* to refer to more than two persons or things.

end (of the day)

HIDEOUS: Farmers are businessmen, *at the end of the day.*
GOOD: Farmers are businessmen, really.

However long this senseless phrase is with us, you should avoid it unless you want to speak in clichés and cotton-wool words.

enjoin on

BAD: I *enjoined on* him to work more efficiently.
GOOD: I enjoined him to work more efficiently.

You can enjoin an action on someone, or enjoin someone to do something, but you cannot enjoin *on* someone to do something.

enormity

BAD: America will not acknowledge the *enormity* of its debts.
GOOD: America will not acknowledge the size of its debts.

Enormity does not mean 'enormousness'. It means the great wickedness of something, such as the enormity of a crime.

entitled to

BAD: You have done the damage and now you are *entitled to* pay for it.
GOOD: You have done the damage and now you are liable to pay for it.

Try not to confuse *entitled*, meaning *having a right to*, with *liable to*, meaning *subject to* or *likely to suffer from*. You can be entitled to compensation, but liable to pay damages.

expect

BAD: We *expect* the work was finished yesterday.
GOOD: We think the work was finished yesterday.

Do not use *expect* in the sense of 'think' and 'suppose' in precise English.

feasible

BAD: It is *feasible* that he got through the door; the lock is broken.
GOOD: It is possible/probable that he got through the door.

Feasible is not a synonym for 'possible' or 'probable'. It means capable of being done, achieved or dealt with: *an improvement in English is feasible.*

forever/for ever

WRONG: I shall be here *forever* if the bus doesn't come.
RIGHT: I shall be here for ever if the bus doesn't come.

WRONG: He was *for ever* complaining about the bus service.
RIGHT: He was forever complaining about the bus service.

Although *forever* is always written as one word in American English, British English distinguishes between the continual sense (*forever*) and the eternal sense (*for ever*). Note this distinction: it is subtle but powerful.

fortuitous

BAD: What a happy coincidence – how *fortuitous!*
GOOD: What a happy coincidence – how fortunate!

Fortuitous does not mean 'fortunate' or 'timely'. It means *accidental, happening by chance*. It may be quite fortuitous that you picked up this book, but it could turn out fortunate!

geriatric

BAD: Aunt Vera is becoming *geriatric;* she can't remember my name.
GOOD: Aunt Vera is becoming forgetful; she can't remember my name.

The noun *geriatrics* describes the medical care of the old. The adjective *geriatric* means *pertaining to the health and welfare of the elderly*. Do not use it to mean 'senile' or 'elderly', or an elderly or senile person.

get

Get is one of the most overused verbs in the language. Use it sparingly in careful English; there are often good equivalents. In particular, make sure you do not use 'have got' for 'have' or 'possess' in formal English.

AVOID: She's *got* three dogs.
BETTER: She has three dogs.

AVOID: We *got* there in good time.
BETTER: We arrived (there) in good time.

AVOID: Will you *get* the prize?
BETTER: Will you win the prize?

AVOID: We've *got* to leave promptly.
BETTER: We must leave promptly.

AVOID: Please *get* the milk on your way back.
BETTER: Please fetch the milk on your way back.

hopefully

BAD: *Hopefully*, everyone will accept this suggestion.
GOOD: One hopes that everyone/With any luck, everyone will accept this suggestion.

The literal meaning of the bad example is *This suggestion will be accepted by everyone in a hopeful manner.* It is of course intended to mean *With any luck ...* or *One hopes that ....* This sense is ubiquitous, but resist it because there are better expressions. The adjective *hopeful* cannot be converted into a sentence adverb and used outside the clause structure to convey the speaker's comment on the statement, like *regrettably* (from regrettable): *Regrettably we cannot accept your application.*

however

CLUMSY: *However,* I must tell you that you are breaking the law.
CLUMSY: I must tell you that you are, *however,* breaking the law.
BETTER: I must, however, tell you that you are breaking the law.

Try not to start a sentence with *however.* Its best position is second in the sentence, after whatever it qualifies (*I must tell you ...*). If placed too far along in the sentence, *however* loses its force and clouds its function.

ilk

BAD: I'm thinking of layabouts, spongers, and people of that *ilk.*
GOOD: I'm thinking of layabouts, spongers, and people of that sort.

Ilk does not mean 'sort' or 'kind'; it is a Scots term, meaning the same *place* or *name,* now usually to be found in a clan chieftain's title.

imply

WRONG: I *imply* from your letter that you think I refused to see him.
RIGHT: I infer from your letter that you think I refused to see him.

Do not confuse *imply* with 'infer'. *Imply* means *suggest,* and need not have as subject a word denoting a person. For the correct use of 'infer' see below.

inasmuch/in so far

WRONG: *In as much* as we are here, we might as well stay.
RIGHT: Inasmuch as we are here, we might as well stay.

WRONG: *Insofar* as we can, we have told you the truth.
RIGHT: In so far as we can, we have told you the truth.

You may have little use for these somewhat pompous-sounding expressions, but if you do write them, write them correctly.

inchoate

BAD: He works in a very erratic, *inchoate* way.
GOOD: He works in an erratic, chaotic way.

Inchoate does not mean 'chaotic' or 'disorganized'. It means *just begun, underdeveloped: an inchoate research project.*

infer

WRONG: Your letter seems to *infer* that I have refused to see him.
RIGHT: Your letter seems to imply/suggest that I have refused to see him.

Do not confuse *infer* with 'imply'. *Infer* means *to draw a conclusion from,* and must have as subject a word denoting a person. For the correct use of 'imply', see above.

in/into

BAD: I have lost my keys and cannot get *in* the house.
GOOD: I have lost my keys and cannot get into the house.

Colloquial English often uses *in* for *into;* avoid this in formal writing.

instigate

BAD: A fresh approach is needed to *instigate* change in the company.
GOOD: A fresh approach is needed to introduce change in the company.

Instigate is not a synonym for 'set up' or 'introduce'. As a specialized legal term it has these meanings, but as a non-technical word it means to *incite* or *urge on:* This book aims to instigate a movement towards better English!

interact

BAD: As a good salesman you must *interact* with your clients.
GOOD: As a good salesman you must impress/please/talk easily with/communicate properly with your clients.

Interact is one of those objectionable foggy neologisms that is intended to substitute for several more precise words. These words are not difficult to find.

involved in

BAD: A person ought to be able to receive medical help without being *involved in* financial anxiety.
GOOD: A person ought to be able to receive medical help without financial anxiety.

The expression *to be involved in* is currently very popular. It is generally quite superfluous, as in this example.

its

WRONG: The dog is chasing *it's* tail.
RIGHT: The dog is chasing its tail.

The possessive pronouns *its, hers, ours, theirs* and *yours* never have an apostrophe. (See also the section on Punctuation.)

it's

WRONG: Yes, *its* certainly a big question.
RIGHT: Yes, it's certainly a big question.

It's meaning *it is* always has an apostrophe.

lay, lie, laid, lain

WRONG: Just *lay* down there./*Lie* her on the sofa.
RIGHT: Just lie down there./Lay her on the sofa.

The verbs *to lay* and *to lie* are often confused. To lay (= to put down, to arrange) is a transitive verb denoting an action performed upon a person or thing; to lie (= to recline, to be situated) is intransitive, describing the action of a person or thing. In these respects they cannot be interchanged.

Note also their past participles. To lay = *laid*; to lie = *lain*:

WRONG: He had *lain* his heart at her feet./He had *laid* on the sand all day.
RIGHT: He had laid his heart at her feet./He had lain on the sand all day.

Further confusion arises out of the past tenses. To lay = *laid*; to lie = *lay*:

WRONG: He *lay(ed)* his heart at her feet./He *laid* on the sand all day.
RIGHT: He laid his heart at her feet./He lay on the sand all day.

Additional points to be aware of are that when *to lie* = *to tell an untruth* it is transitive and has *lied* as both past participle and past tense, and that when *to lay* = *to produce eggs* or *to wager* it is intransitive and has *laid* as both past participle and past tense.

leading question

BAD: I'll test him with a *leading question* which he probably won't be able to answer.
GOOD: I'll test him with a searching question which he probably won't be able to answer.

A *leading question* is not a searching question or the most important question. It is a legal term describing a question so phrased that it prompts the person to give the desired answer.

less/fewer

WRONG: *Less* than twenty people attended the meeting.
RIGHT: Fewer than twenty people attended the meeting.

When you are talking of actual numbers, use *fewer*, not *less*. When you are talking of amounts, use *less*: The baby weighed *less* than *four pounds*.

liable to

WRONG: This football ground is *liable to* be chosen for the next match.
RIGHT: This football ground is likely to be chosen for the next match.

Liable to meaning 'likely to' is American English.

lie: see lay, lie, laid, lain

likewise

BAD: He looked thin and unshaven, *likewise* his clothes were torn and dirty.
GOOD: He looked thin and unshaven, and his clothes were torn and dirty.

Do not use *likewise* as the conjunction 'and' or 'also'. It is an adverb meaning *in the same or similar manner*, or *moreover*. For example: *He was rude to me, and treated her likewise.*

literally

BAD: Dropping litter has *literally* become the disease of the nation.
GOOD: Dropping litter has become the disease of the nation.

Using *literally* as an intensifying adverb often has the opposite effect. It weakens the sense by suggesting that the meaning is in fact not literally true, but a self-conscious figure of speech; *literally* itself is being used as a figure of speech. When *literally* is omitted, the figure of speech can speak directly.

locate

BAD: He asked the secretary to *locate* his accountant.
GOOD: He asked the secretary to find his accountant.

You *locate* somebody or something if you aim above all to discover the <u>place</u> where the object of your search is. You *find* somebody or something if your aim is to discover the object <u>wherever</u> it may be. For example, you could locate this information by looking up 'locate' in the index.

may/might

WRONG: He *may* never have found the house, but for getting lost on Dartmoor.
RIGHT: He might never have found the house, but for getting lost on Dartmoor.

The past tense of *may* is *might*. The sentence above describes an event that has happened and therefore *may*, the present tense, cannot be used. If there is uncertainty about whether the event has happened or not – *He may have found the house, I don't know yet* – then either *may* or *might* is acceptable.

means

BAD: The law allows a citizen to defend himself by *every means* that *are* allowed by law.

GOOD: The law allows a citizen to defend himself by every means that is allowed by law/every means allowed by law.

Means used in the sense of something by which a result is achieved may be used either as a singular noun or as a plural one. But beware of mixing the two; *every means* (singular) should not be followed by *are* (plural).

mitigate

WRONG: This blunder will *mitigate* against his chances of promotion.

RIGHT: This blunder will militate against his chances of promotion.

The malapropism *mitigate* for *militate* is strangely common. Mitigate means alleviate, appease, moderate: *Nothing can mitigate the brutality of his crime.* Militate means to serve as a strong influence against.

moment (in time)

HORRIBLE: At this *moment in time* the situation is very delicate.

GOOD: At the moment/at present the situation is very delicate.

At this moment in time is another cotton-wool phrase, like *at the end of the day*, which is as pompous as it is meaningless.

motivated

BAD: She was obviously *motivated* to check the results very carefully.

GOOD: She obviously wanted to check the results very carefully.

Use *motivated* and *motivation* with caution if you do not want to think of people as mechanical systems, who do not have wants or desires but are merely programmed, 'motivated'.

mutual

BAD: Sarah is the *mutual* friend of both brothers.

BETTER: Sarah is the friend of both brothers.

Mutual meaning 'in common' is quite accepted now, but it does not mean this. *Mutual* describes a reciprocal relationship between two people or things: the mutual affection between mother and child is the affection felt by each towards the other. *Mutual friend* suggests that there is a reciprocal relationship between the two brothers, but they might be enemies.

nature

BAD: The silly *nature* of that child always amuses me.
BETTER: The silliness of that child always amuses me.

The meaning is more direct if you avoid using an adjective plus *nature* as a roundabout way of saying an abstract noun.

negotiate

BAD: Will he be able to *negotiate* the difficulty?
GOOD: Will he be able to overcome the difficulty?

Negotiate is not a synonym for 'overcome'. It means to hold a discussion so as to reach an agreement, to make an arrangement by such a discussion: *The union negotiated a pay rise with management.*

neither (1)

WRONG: *Neither* man *are* honest and neither of them is clever.
RIGHT: Neither man is honest and neither of them is clever.

Neither is always singular, both as an adjective and a pronoun.

neither (2)

WRONG: I don't want any of your excuses *neither.*
RIGHT: I don't want any of your excuses either.

Do not use *neither* to emphasize a preceding negative.

neurotic

BAD: He is *neurotic* – so nervous and indecisive.
GOOD: He is so nervous and indecisive.

Like 'schizophrenic', *neurotic* is an overused psychiatric term, and usually suggests that the speaker cannot be bothered to think of a more appropriate word. A genuine neurosis is a mental disturbance characterized by a state of unconscious conflict, usually accompanied by anxiety and obsessional fears – an illness which should not be confused with such everyday vices as timorousness and inconsistency.

nice

OFTEN: What a *nice* day!/We had a *nice* meal./He is a *nice* person.
BETTER: What a lovely day!/We had a delicious meal./He is a delightful person.

Nice meaning *pleasant*, etc. is a loose definition; it is one of the most over-worked words in the language. Use it sparingly. Nice may legitimately mean subtle, requiring precision, care, tact or discrimination: *A nice question; a nice point.*

none the less

WRONG: *Nonetheless*, I shall do as I promised.
RIGHT: *None the less*, I shall do as I promised.

Although you will often see the one-word spelling, the three-word spelling is correct.

notice

WRONG: I've spilt soup on my tie but it won't notice.
RIGHT: I've spilt soup on my tie but it won't show.

It is wrong to use the transitive verb *to notice* here, instead of the intransitive *to show* (= to be visible).

obligate

WRONG: I am *obligated* to resign.
RIGHT: I am obliged to resign.

Obligate is a legal term and should never be used as a synonym for 'oblige'.

off of

WRONG: John fell *off of* the ladder.

RIGHT: John fell off the ladder.

Off makes *of* superfluous and incorrect.

ongoing

BAD: This is an *ongoing* situation that is likely to continue.
GOOD: This situation is likely to continue.

Ongoing as an adjective meaning *that goes on* has a valid use – a problem may be ongoing. But an 'ongoing situation that is likely to continue' is both tautologous and a cliché.

only

BAD: He *only* told me part of the truth.
BAD: The dog *only* had three legs.
BAD: You *only* have to ask, and we will help you.

GOOD: He told me only part of the truth.
GOOD: The dog had only three legs.
GOOD: You have only to ask, and we will help you.

We should always make it clear that *only* describes only what comes immediately after it, but it is easy to be careless. Precise use makes for more effective expression.

onto/on to

BAD: I held *onto* the railing as I crossed the bridge.
GOOD: I held on to the railing as I crossed the bridge.

Onto is an American spelling which is taking over in Britain. Don't let it.

orient(ate)

POSSIBLE: This method of teaching is *oriented* towards the slower learners.
BETTER: This method of teaching is orientated towards the slower learners.

Orient and *orientate* are synonymous. The latter sounds pleasanter and is therefore preferable. Similarly, dissociate is preferable to disassociate, educationist to educationalist and racist to racialist.

other than

WRONG: I can't believe your explanation *other than* cautiously.
RIGHT: I can't believe your explanation otherwise than/except cautiously.

Other than is not an adverb, it has an adjectival function only. It can be used only where 'other' is an adjective or pronoun: *I would prefer some other colour than that one.*

otherwise

WRONG: This is the inevitable result of decline, economic or *otherwise.*
WRONG: No one, pickets or *otherwise,* should behave like that.
WRONG: What is worrying us is his hypocrisy or *otherwise.*

RIGHT: This is the inevitable result of decline, economic or other.
RIGHT: No one, pickets or others, should behave like that.
RIGHT: What is worrying us is his hypocrisy.

Otherwise is an adverb; it cannot be used as an adjective or noun. If the correct form sounds awkward, then there should be an alternative way of expressing the same sentiment: *Whether it is economic or not, this is .../ Whether they are pickets or not, no one .../... his hypocrisy – or whatever there is about him that makes us suspect he's insincere.*

overall

BAD: Every point in the report impressed him. *Overall,* he was very pleased with it.
GOOD: Every point in the report impressed him and he was very pleased with it.

Overall is almost always superfluous and rarely necessary. In this example it is redundant because the first sentence indicates that all aspects of the report have pleased him, and *overall* merely repeats the idea.

overly

WRONG: I wasn't *overly* surprised to hear it.
RIGHT: I wasn't too surprised to hear it.

Overly for *excessively* is American English, and you should use *excessively, too,* or *over-*.

overview

BAD: Let me give you an *overview* of what this machine can do.
GOOD: Let me give you an explanation of what this machine can do.

A jargon word of the worst kind. There are several preferable equivalents: *explanation, report* or *survey.*

parameter

BAD: You can't judge modern painting by classical *parameters.*
GOOD: You can't judge modern painting by classical criteria.

Try not to use *parameter* as a synonym for 'criterion'. *Parameter* is a precise term for a constant in a mathematical expression, such as a and b in algebraic formulae. It is best left to those who will treat it with respect.

pathetic

BAD: Your argument is *pathetic.*
GOOD: Your argument is very poor/does not stand up/is absurd, etc.

The colloquial meaning of *pathetic* for 'bad' or 'miserably inadequate' causes the true meaning of pathetic (exciting pity) to be neglected. Try to find an equivalent for the colloquial meaning of *pathetic* rather than lose a valuable word in the language.

personally

BAD: I *personally* think that it's wrong.
GOOD: I think it's wrong (myself).

Personally means literally *in person.* Used with personal pronouns, it is inevitably tautologous, for if I am talking about myself there is no need to refer to myself in person. *Personally* tries to sound authoritative, but tends to sound pompous.

plus

BAD: You will speak good English. *Plus* you will learn to be discriminating and precise.
GOOD: You will speak good English. In addition you will learn/You will also learn to be discriminating and precise.

Plus used as 'in addition to' is an unacceptable American colloquialism.

portentous

BAD: His conversation was *portentous,* slow-witted and dull.
GOOD: His conversation was solemn, slow-witted and dull.

The primary meaning of *portentous* is not 'ponderous and solemn', but *like a portent, ominous,* or *prodigious.* If its secondary meaning is overused then its most important meaning will be forgotten, and more suitable equivalents like *solemn* will be neglected.

position in regard to

BAD: The *position in regard to* social benefits is now critical.
GOOD: The state of social benefits is now critical.

Position in regard to is ugly and not difficult to avoid.

prefer than

WRONG: I prefer apples *than* pears.
WRONG: He preferred to go to prison *than* pay the fine.

RIGHT: I prefer apples to pears.
RIGHT: He preferred to go to prison rather than pay the fine.

You do not *prefer* something 'than' something else, but *to* something else. You do not *prefer to do* something 'than' something else, you *prefer to do* something *rather* than something else.

presently

BAD: This musician is *presently* being acclaimed as a genius.
GOOD: This musician is now being acclaimed as a genius.

Presently meaning at *present, currently* is long-established American English. It has a slightly precious ring to it and has no advantages over *currently* or *now.* It is also often used euphemistically in English: *'We will take you to be X-rayed presently'* is likely to mean that the unfortunate patient must look forward to a long wait.

prioritize

BAD: We must *prioritize* the needs of handicapped children.
GOOD: We must give priority to the needs of handicapped children.

And we must fight the growing tendency, influenced by America, towards jargonized (see how easy it is!) shorthand. Some examples, like *privatized*, have come into the language to fill a genuine need (try expressing its meaning in fewer than five words). Others, like this one, which telescopes a succinct phrasal verb, should be resisted.

prior to

BAD: *Prior to* going out, she phoned her accountant.
GOOD: Before going out, she phoned her accountant.

This is another Americanism. The philosophy seems to be: if one word will do, use at least two. Don't!

pristine

BAD: She was wearing a *pristine* new dress.
GOOD: She was wearing a spotless new dress.

Pristine means the opposite of 'new', 'fresh' or 'pure'; it means *ancient* or *original*, or *having its original unspoilt condition.*

proven

BAD: Applicants must be able to offer *proven* experience of management.
GOOD: Applicants must be able to offer experience of management.

Proven is generally superfluous, and here it makes the sense tautological: experience is in itself a proof, so proven experience is a tautology.

provided that

WRONG: He would not have caught pneumonia *provided that* he had worn a coat.
RIGHT: He would not have caught pneumonia if he had worn a coat.

Provided that is often used mistakenly for 'if'. Keep it for a true stipulation: *He said he would be punctual, provided that the trains were running on time.*

question (of being)

BAD: What is important is the *question of being* there to represent the chairman.
GOOD: What is important is to be there to represent the chairman.

It is not a question at all. The phrase *the question of being* merely means *to be*. Reserve the word *question* for things which require answers.

quite

WRONG: The general did not quite command the army for the entire campaign.
RIGHT: The general did not command the army for the entire campaign.

Here, *quite* is intended to qualify *the entire*, not *command* (which makes it seem that he was not wholly in command). 'Quite the entire', however, is tautologous (= 'entirely the entire'), so omit *quite*.

re

BAD: We want to hold an emergency meeting *re* the secretary's resignation.
GOOD: We want to hold an emergency meeting about/to discuss the secretary's resignation.

Re is a legal term best left to lawyers. It can be replaced, with much better result, by either *about* or a suitable verb.

redundant

POSSIBLE: His argument was *redundant* in the context.
BETTER: His argument was superfluous/inappropriate in the context.

Although *redundant* is accepted as a synonym for *superfluous*, it would be a pity to lose the distinctions in meaning between the two words. It is preferable to confine *redundant* to employees who have been dismissed because there is no longer work for them to do.

replica(te)

WRONG: The boys made a *replica* of the space shuttle 'Challenger'.
RIGHT: The boys made a model of the space shuttle 'Challenger'.

BAD: We fully intend to *replicate* the policy of the previous study-group.
GOOD: We fully intend to continue the policy of the previous study-group.

A *replica* is, properly, a work of art which has been copied by the original artist; hence it has come to mean any object copied by its creator, not by others. The word *replica* should not be used as a synonym for 'repetition' (as in *His speech seemed a replica of the one he made last year*), and you should avoid the Americanism *replicate*.

request

BAD: I *requested* him not to smoke in my office.
GOOD: I asked him not to smoke in my office.

Request is not a polite way of saying *ask*; this is a clumsy and incorrect usage which is gaining ground in our increasingly euphemistic society. To request means to ask *for* – if I said he had requested a cigarette in my office, I should be on firmer linguistic ground in describing my refusal!

resentful at

WRONG: I was resentful *at* his behaviour.
RIGHT: I was resentful *of* his behaviour.

Resentful is always followed by *of*.

respectively

WRONG: John Gielgud and Laurence Olivier *respectively* are famous actors.
RIGHT: John Gielgud and Laurence Olivier are famous actors.

WRONG: He is a barrister and an M.P. *respectively*.
RIGHT: He is (both) a barrister and an M.P.

Respectively has one correct use only: to link up subjects or objects in a clear way where more than one is the subject or object of a single verb. For example, in *Cats and horses eat meat and grass respectively*, the use of *respectively* indicates which animal eats what. Very often, the word is used superfluously – this is its most common misuse, as shown in the first example above. The second shows *respectively* wrongly used for *both*.

return

WRONG: He returned it *back* to me.
RIGHT: He returned it to me.

Returning something means giving back something, so there is no need for *back*.

scarcely

WRONG: He had *scarcely* finished the conversation *than* she entered the room.
RIGHT: He had scarcely finished the conversation when she entered the room./No sooner had he finished the conversation than she entered the room.

Scarcely cannot be regarded as a comparative like 'no sooner', so it cannot be followed by *than*.

scenario

WRONG: The usual *scenario* was going on between the couple upstairs; shouts and thumps could be heard through the ceiling.
RIGHT: The usual scene was going on between the couple upstairs; shouts and thumps could be heard through the ceiling.

Do not use *scenario* as a synonym for 'scene' or 'situation'. It has a specific meaning to describe the outline of the plot of a play or film script with the details of scenes, stage directions, etc.

schizophrenic

BAD: I feel quite *schizophrenic* about whether or not to go.
GOOD: I'm in two minds/I don't know whether or not to go.

Like 'neurotic', *schizophrenic* is an overused and misused psychiatric term. Schizophrenia is a devastating illness characterized by hallucinations, delusions, etc., and is not, as popularly misconceived, a simple 'split personality', nor can it be trivialized to mere indecision.

serendipity

WRONG: It was a *serendipitous* moment when he at last found the letter after searching all day for it.
RIGHT: It was a lucky moment when he at last found the letter after searching all day for it.

Serendipity is the act of making pleasant discoveries by accident, or the fact or knack of doing this. If the search has been deliberate, then the discovery cannot be serendipitous. The word is not a synonym for 'fortunate' or 'lucky'.

shall

CARELESS: I/We *will* phone you tomorrow. (expressing simple fact)
GOOD: I/We shall phone you tomorrow.

CARELESS: He/You/They *will* try harder tomorrow. (expressing determination)
GOOD: He/You/They shall try harder tomorrow.

There are useful distinctions in meaning between *shall* and *will*, although nowadays *will* tends to take the place of both. It would impoverish the language to let these shades of meaning die out. *I shall* and *we shall* express the simple future: *We shall see the house after the next turning.* If you want to express intention or determination, use *I will, we will*: *I will revise thoroughly for the exam.* For the second and third persons, singular and plural (you, he, she, it, they) the rule is exactly the converse. *You/he/she/it/ they shall* expresses intention or determination, *you/he/she/it/they will* expresses the simple future. *Would* and *should* follow exactly the same rule.

simplistic

POSSIBLE: It was a *simplistic* argument.
BETTER: It was an oversimplified argument.

Simplistic, like many other technical words and jargon, has long gained a foothold in the language. In formal writing especially, *oversimplified* is preferable.

since

WRONG: It is hardly four years ago *since* we were last discussing it.
RIGHT: It is hardly four years since we were last discussing it./It is hardly four years ago that we ...

'Ago' used with *since* repeats the same idea.

situation

BAD: This is a war *situation*.
GOOD: This is a war.

An attributive noun in place of an adjective before *situation* makes for very ugly expression and enervates the language. Like 'motivation', *situation* suggests that human behaviour is mechanical, being in a situation that induces a certain response.

substantial

WRONG: Tax increases are making a *substantial* hole in the public's pocket.
RIGHT: Tax increases are making a large hole in the public's pocket.

Substantial is not a synonym for 'large'. It means *of substance, actually existing, of solid material, having much, in essentials.* Most of these senses are incongruous if used to describe the figure of speech 'to make a hole in the pocket'. A hole cannot be made of solid material – but one can owe the taxman a substantial sum of money.

substitute

WRONG: They *substituted* the old piano by a new one.
RIGHT: They substituted a new piano for the old one./They replaced the old piano by/with a new one.

Do not confuse the two idioms *substitute for* and *replace by/with.*

superior

WRONG: Once again he showed that he was *superior than* all his competitors.
RIGHT: Once again he showed that he was superior to all his competitors.

Superior than is the wrong idiom. Something can only be superior *to* something else.

this

BAD: I asked *this* man who was waiting for a bus what the time was.
GOOD: I asked a man who was waiting for a bus what the time was.

This is often substituted for *a* in conversation when the object described is more vivid to the speaker than to the listener. It is an irritating and incorrect expression.

transpire

WRONG: What *transpired* between the two brothers is still a mystery.
RIGHT: What happened between the two brothers is still a mystery.

Do not use *transpire* in place of 'happen' or 'come about'. Its proper figurative sense is *to leak out, to come to be known.* The literal meaning is *to give off as vapour, exhale* or *to emit through the skin.* It could, of course, transpire that one brother murdered the other.

under way/underway

BAD: The play got *underway* half an hour late.
GOOD: The play got under way half an hour late.

Under way is written as two words in British English. *Underway* is the American English spelling.

unique

WRONG: The weather that summer was *unique.*
RIGHT: The weather that summer was extraordinary.

WRONG: It was rather *unique.*
RIGHT: It was rather unusual/remarkable.

If something is *unique,* then it is the only one of its kind in existence. Do not use the word to describe rarity or excellence. Summer weather cannot be unique; however glorious or dreadful, there will always be another summer with comparable weather. An object cannot be *rather* unique; either it is unique, or it is not.

universally

WRONG: His motion was *universally* rejected by *all.*
RIGHT: His motion was universally rejected./His motion was rejected by all.

Universally and *all* have the same meaning and so, used together, are tautologous.

up (until)

BAD: *Up* until yesterday, the weather was fine.
GOOD: Until yesterday, the weather was fine.

The conjunction *until* makes *up* superfluous and incorrect.

Grammatical bad habits

The first section of this book deals with bad habits in the language we speak, words which we are continually misusing. Some of the commonest grammatical mistakes are also included. This next section gives examples of bad habits in grammar, for example using a plural verb with a singular noun. Grammatical terms are used because, although they may be unfamiliar to the reader, explanations become unnecessarily long if one tries to avoid them. They are explained on pages 116–131. Like many taboos, the taboo about grammar is unreasonable; we describe the engine of a car using technical terms, so why can't we do the same when describing the components of a sentence? This section may be more useful to students for whom English is a second language, although the mistakes illustrated are continually being demonstrated by English people too.

Agreement (between verb and subject)

(1)

WRONG: The whole range of mountains *are* visible from the sea.
WRONG: Neither of the men *were* very sympathetic to us.
WRONG: *Are* either of these bags yours?

In the above examples the verb should be in the singular, because the subject (*range, neither* of the men, *either* of these bags) is in the singular. A verb agrees in number (and person) with its subject.

RIGHT: The whole range of mountains *is* visible from the sea.
RIGHT: Neither of the men *was* very sympathetic to us.
RIGHT: *Is* either of these bags yours?

(2)

WRONG: On his desk *was* a book and a bundle of papers.
WRONG: The minister, with his delegates, *were* warmly received.
WRONG: His son, as well as mine, *are* playing for the school.

When a verb has two subjects connected by *and*, the verb is plural. When a singular subject has attached to it a phrase introduced by *with* or *as well as*, the verb is singular.

RIGHT: On his desk *were* a book and a bundle of papers.
RIGHT: The minister, with his delegates, *was* warmly received.

RIGHT: His son, as well as mine, *is* playing for the school.

(3)

WRONG: Either your director or his manager *have* made an error.
WRONG: Neither Paul nor John *know* anything about it.

Two singular subjects separated by *either ... or, neither ... nor* take a singular verb.

RIGHT: Either your director or his manager *has* made an error.
RIGHT: Neither Paul nor John *knows* anything about it.

(4)

WRONG: Neither Peter nor his sisters *was* present.
WRONG: Neither Richard nor I *has* replied to the letter.

If the subjects separated by *neither ... nor* are of different number or person, the verb agrees with the nearest subject (*sisters* and *I*).

RIGHT: Neither Peter nor his sisters *were* present.
RIGHT: Neither Richard nor I *have* replied to the letter.

(5)

WRONG: Everybody has *their* failings.
WRONG: Nobody in *their* right mind would dream of doing it.
WRONG: Each pupil tried *their* hardest.

Everybody, each, every, nobody and *anybody* must be followed by verbs, pronouns and adjectives in the singular.

RIGHT: Everybody has *his* failings.
RIGHT: Nobody in *his* right mind would dream of doing it.
RIGHT: Each pupil tried *his/her* hardest.

Despite the current trend towards being even-handed in matters regarding gender, sometimes to the point of absurdity, there really is no need to put '*her* failings', '*her* right mind' (unless the context is quite plainly an all-female one – pupils at a girls' school, where each tried *her* hardest).

(6)

WRONG: The two sisters hate *one another.*
WRONG: Do animals love *each other?*

Each other is used when we speak of two persons or things, *one another* when we speak of more than two.

RIGHT: The two sisters hate *each other.*
RIGHT: Do animals love *one another?*

(7)

WRONG: Each boy and girl *have* received a souvenir.
WRONG: Every book and every manuscript *have* been entered in our catalogue.

If the subject consists of two or more singular nouns connected by *and,* and preceded by *each* or *every,* the verb is in the singular.

RIGHT: Each boy and girl *has* received a souvenir.
RIGHT: Every book and every manuscript *has* been entered in our catalogue.

(8)

WRONG: This is one of the best books that *has* been written on the subject.
WRONG: He was one of the greatest philosophers that *has* ever lived.

In the above sentences the subject of *have been written* and *have ever lived* is *that.* It is plural because its antecedents, *books* and *philosophers,* are plural. A relative pronoun agrees in number with its antecedent.

RIGHT: This is one of the best books that *have* been written on the subject.
RIGHT: He was one of the greatest philosophers that *have* ever lived.

Also

BAD: We did not want to go into the question, *also* we were too busy with other things.

Also is an adverb, not a conjunction. It is used to link sentences in speech, but avoid this usage in writing.

GOOD: We did not want to go into the question; *and* we were *also/moreover,* we were too busy with other things.

Articles

WRONG: She was wearing an old and *a* tawdry dress.

The article (*a, an, the*) need not be repeated when only one person or thing is referred to.

RIGHT: She was wearing an old and tawdry dress.

Collective nouns

WRONG: This *meeting* approves of the suggestion made by *their* chairman.
WRONG: The *Cabinet* was summoned for ten o'clock, when *they* met at Downing Street.

WRONG: The *committee* do not agree, although *it is* unwilling to reject the offer altogether.

A collective noun is generally singular. It may, however, take a plural verb if the sense suggests a body consisting of several individuals, rather than considered as a whole.

Collective nouns should not be made singular in one part of the sentence and plural in the other.

RIGHT: This meeting approves of the suggestion made by *its* chairman. (Or *approve ... their.*)

RIGHT: The Cabinet was summoned for ten o'clock, when *it* met at Downing Street. (Or *were summoned ... they.*)

RIGHT: The committee do not agree, although *they are* unwilling to reject the offer altogether. (Or *does not ... it is.*)

Comparatives and superlatives

(1)
WRONG: St Peter's at Rome is larger than *any* church.
WRONG: St Peter's at Rome is the largest of *all other* churches.

In the first example, St Peter's is included in *any* church. *Other* must be added. In the second example, St Peter's is excluded by the word *other*. *Other* must be omitted.

RIGHT: St Peter's at Rome is larger than *any other* church.
RIGHT: St Peter's at Rome is the largest of *all* churches.

(2)
WRONG: Sarah is the *prettiest* of the two sisters.

When <u>two</u> persons or things are compared, the comparative, not the superlative, should be used.

RIGHT: Sarah is the *prettier* of the two sisters.

Gerunds

(1)
WRONG: You cannot forbid *him* leaving.
WRONG: What is the use of *you* trying to threaten him?

The object of *forbid* is *leaving*, not *him*. *Leaving* is therefore a gerund or verb-noun, not a participle or verb-adjective. An adjective cannot be the object of a noun. Because *leaving* is a noun it must be qualified by a possessive adjective (my, your, his, her, our, your, their), not by the pronoun *him*.

In the second example the preposition *of* should govern *trying*, instead of *you*. The question is asking 'What is the use of trying?' not 'What is the use of you?' Again the sense requires a gerund (*trying*) preceded by the possessive adjective *your*.

RIGHT: You cannot forbid *his* leaving.
RIGHT: What is the use of *your* trying to threaten him?

(2)
WRONG: You have worsened *instead of improved* the situation.

Instead of must be followed by a gerund, not by a past participle.

RIGHT: You have worsened the situation *instead of improving* it.

He or him? She or her?

WRONG: If you were *him*, what would you do?

This is a very common error. The subject of the sentence is *you*, so the pronoun should agree with the subject; *him* would agree with the object. Colloquial expressions such as 'It's me', 'It's him' are acceptable, although strictly speaking they should read 'It's I', 'It's he', etc., as they are the subject of the verb.

RIGHT: If you were *he*, what would you do?

I or me?

WRONG: They told my brother and *I* to leave at once.
WRONG: Between you and *I*, she is not very clever.

Prepositions and transitive verbs always take an object after them, not a subject.

RIGHT: They told my brother and *me* to leave at once.
RIGHT: Between you and *me*, she is not very clever.

Participles

BAD: His last *days* were spent in Paris, *working* for a publishing firm.

BAD: *Having finished* the page, *the book* was shut.

BAD: *Hearing* the noise, *the thought* crossed my mind that there were burglars in the house.

A participle should be clearly related to the noun or pronoun it is meant to qualify. Although the sense is clear in these examples, the participles are not correctly related to their proper nouns or pronouns. Grammatically, *working* refers to *days* in the first example, which cannot make sense, for it is people, not days, who work. The second example suggests that once the book had finished the page, it was shut (when of course it is an unmentioned reader who finished the page). *The thought* is made the subject in the third example. Thoughts cannot hear noises, so this must be wrong. It is not difficult to avoid these very frequent errors.

RIGHT: His last days were spent in Paris, *where he worked* for a publishing firm.

RIGHT: *When the page was finished,* the book was shut./*Having finished* the page, *I* (*he, you,* etc.) shut the book.

RIGHT: *Hearing* the noise, *I* wondered whether there were burglars in the house.

When the noun or pronoun and the participle have no grammatical connection with the rest of the sentence, then the participle need <u>not</u> be clearly related:

This being the case, let's go now./Weather permitting, we want to go sailing./All things considered, let's be discreet.

Relative pronouns

WRONG: He wrote a rude reply *but which* he soon regretted having sent.

WRONG: We found a firm which had a large quantity of window frames *and which* they could not sell.

And or *but* should not be used before a relative pronoun (*who, which, that, what*). In the first example, it is also correct to keep *but* and omit the relative pronoun.

RIGHT: He wrote a rude reply, *which* he soon regretted having sent/*but* he soon regretted having sent it.

RIGHT: We found a firm which had a large quantity of window frames *which* they could not sell.

Tenses

(1)

WRONG: I *should have like to have gone,* but I was not able to.

WRONG: I *intended to have gone,* but I was not able to.

WRONG: I was very annoyed with him, and I *should like to have prevented* his extravagance.

When the main verb already contains *have,* as in *should have liked* in the first example, there is no need to use the perfect infinitive – *to have gone.* The idea of non-fulfilment is already implied in the main verb. After the past tenses of *intend, hope, expect,* etc., the use of the present infinitive – *to go* – is again preferred, but the perfect infinitive is also acceptable. In the third example, the *have* must go with the main verb and not with the infinitive.

RIGHT: I *should have liked to go,* but I was not able to.

RIGHT: I *intended to go/to have gone,* but I was not able to.

RIGHT: I was very annoyed with him, and *should have liked to prevent* his extravagance.

(2)

WRONG: We should be very grateful if you *will* answer immediately.

WRONG: We shall be very happy if you *would* stay with us.

If *should* or *would* is used in a main clause, *shall* and *will* must not be used in the dependent clause or clauses, and vice versa.

RIGHT: We should be very grateful if you *would* answer immediately.

RIGHT: We shall be very happy if you *will* stay with us.

Who or whom?

WRONG: This is the work of a musician *whom* is hailed as a genius.

WRONG: *Whom* do you think wrote to me yesterday?

Whom would be correct if it referred to the object of the verb; but in both cases it is referring to the subject of the verb – the musician and the person who wrote the letter. The only correct form, therefore, is *who.*

RIGHT: This is the work of a musician *who* they say is a genius.

RIGHT: *Who* do you think wrote to me yesterday?

Redundant words and phrases

'Go along until you reach a kind of turning on the left.' If this instruction was written down, nine times out of ten the *kind of* would be omitted, unless the turning was very unusual. There are countless words and phrases in speech which serve no useful purpose and would be omitted in writing. They tend to slip in unthinkingly, and while they might pad out a sentence they also clutter it up and make tedious listening for others.

It would, of course, be extremely difficult never to use some of these words; everyone, except perhaps trained speakers, uses *um* and *er*. However, many of them can be erased with practice, making the way you talk much more clear and expressive. Simply talking a little more slowly gives you more time to think about what you are saying.

Some of the phrases listed below have been mentioned in the **Bad habits** section, for this is exactly what they are. Some of them are also included in **Clichés**.

actually
and so on and so forth
arguably
as such
at the end of the day
at this moment in time

basically
broadly speaking
by and large

comparatively

definitely

I mean
if you like
in a way
in essence
in the event
in (actual) fact
in the final analysis
in the order of

in terms of

kind of

meaningful

necessarily

particularly

real
relatively
respectively

situation (plus noun: for example *We are facing a crisis situation*)
sort of

undue

virtually

what can only be described as
when all's said and done

you know

To illustrate how these redundant words and phrases may be discarded, read the following extract. Then read it again, omitting those in italics; see how unnecessary they are, and how much better the piece is without them.

Telling you how to mend a puncture is *actually* not what I'm supposed to be doing; I should be talking about 'A visit to the dentist' *and so on and so forth*, but it could be said that plugging holes in teeth is *arguably* quite similar to plugging holes in tyres. I don't think there's any rubber involved in dentistry, *as such*, but *at the end of the day* the results are similar. *At this moment in time* I've no dental qualifications but maybe at the end of my talk you'll think I deserve them. *Basically* I'm a cyclist, not a medical man – although *broadly speaking* there's a good chance that most doctors and dentists can ride a bike, *by and large* not so many bikers are able to set a broken leg or extract a wisdom tooth.

American English

Languages are continually borrowing from each other, and English has adopted countless words and expressions which originate from America. Many of them have been welcomed, like *teenager* and *commuter*, and American colloquialisms and slang (characteristically vigorous and witty) are always popular. However, we should make an effort to resist some of these borrowings – and it takes an effort when we see and hear them all around us, used by the media, politicians and even respected writers. There is no good reason why such words should oust those which they seek to replace.

You will find the American cliché 'No way!' in the section on **Clichés**, while the following very common Americanisms are illustrated in **Bad habits**:

alright
anymore/anytime
different than
due to
forever
hopefully
liable to
obligate
onto
overly
overview
plus
presently
prior to
underway

For these, and for all the further examples given below, a more effective British English equivalent exists.

all of

BAD: *All of* the children were there.
GOOD: All the children were there.

Good English does not place *all of* before nouns to mean *the whole of, the entirety*. It is quite usual to place *all of* before pronouns, e.g. *All of us were there*, but before nouns all that is needed is *all*.

as from

BAD: *As from* June 5th strawberries will be on sale.
GOOD: From June 5th strawberries will be on sale.

As from preceding a date which has passed is acceptable, but not before a future date.

contact

BAD: He will *contact* you as soon as possible.
GOOD: He will write to/telephone you as soon as possible.

This shorthand word for several methods of communication has long been accepted. The objection to it is that, however convenient, it is a very impersonal word.

doubt that

BAD: I *doubt that* they will be excused.
GOOD: I doubt whether/if they will be excused.

If the sentence began *I have no doubt* ... then that would be correct. But after a positive statement the English idiom takes *whether* or *if*.

like (as a conjunction)

BAD: They all talked incessantly - *like* people do after a shock.
GOOD: They all talked incessantly - as people do after a shock.

Do not use *like* as a conjunction, except informally.

meaningful

BAD: They agreed it had been a constructive, *meaningful* discussion.
GOOD: They agreed it had been a constructive discussion.

Meaningful is generally a superfluous and <u>meaningless</u> word.

Phrasal verbs

English abounds with phrasal verbs. Take the verb *to break*, for instance: to break *down*, to break *into*, to break *through*, to break *off* are given different meanings by the use of distinct adverbial particles with the simple verb. However, phrasal verbs are useful only if they do mean something distinct from the simple verb – if they do not, they merely clutter up a sentence. There are many such phrasal verbs in American English which are gaining acceptability in British English:

check *up on*
close *down* (when used to mean *to close,* not to close down entirely)
consult *with*
face *up to*
go *up*
lose *out on*
match *up*
meet *up with*
miss *out on*
sound *out*
start *up*
stop *off*
try *out*
visit *with*

These adverbs and prepositions do not intensify the meaning of the verbs, as is sometimes thought. If they do anything, they weaken the force of the verbs. All these verbs do their job better if left alone.

Subjunctive

POSSIBLE: I suggest that the boy *be* sent home.
BETTER: I suggest that the boy should be/is sent home.

Using the subjective in *that*-clauses after words expressing command, hope, intention, wish, etc., used to be restricted to very formal language in English. It is, however, a very common American usage which has now gained a foothold here. There is no need to use the subjunctive unless the context is very formal; it can give an inappropriate tone of stiffness. *Should* or *may* with the infinitive, or the ordinary indicative (in informal language) sounds more natural in English.

Clichés

Clichés are phrases which have become worn out and ineffective through overuse. They are the 'convenience food' of English. They are ready-made – the language is *chock-a-block* with these overused phrases. And, like tinned and frozen food which you can eat in minutes, they do their job quickly; clichés are, *to all intents and purposes,* a common language, readily understood by all. Should they *drive us up the wall,* or are they *a blessing in disguise?*

You should be cautious about using clichés for two important reasons: one, they generally sound superficial and inadequate when used in a formal context; two, they do not carry strong meaning, because they have been exhausted through overuse. Never use them in formal writing.

There is, however, a lot of unnecessary snobbery about clichés. Sometimes they can be useful and not to use them would mean very lengthy explanations. They can be used to sound generally agreeable in conversation, or, if used ironically, for humour.

Here are some of the most common clichés.

ad nauseam
alive and kicking
at the end of the day

ball game
blessing in disguise
blind as a bat
bone of contention

castles in Spain
chop and change
climate of opinion
cool as a cucumber
crème de la crème

in this day and age
draw a veil
drive up the wall

fair and square

the fair sex
in the final analysis
finger in every pie
within the framework

green with envy
for good and all
grind to a halt

halcyon days
heart and soul
take it to heart
high and dry

(to all) intents and purposes

last but not least
leave no stone unturned
leave severely alone

mists of time
at this moment (or point) in time

name of the game
no way!

of that ilk
old as the hills

part and parcel
powers that be

rat race

safe and sound
slow but sure

thick and thin
thin end of the wedge
tip of the iceberg

ugly as sin
up with the lark

ways and means
white elephant
wind of change

Split infinitives

A split infinitive occurs when *to* is separated from the infinitive by an adverb or adverbial phrase. It used to be considered the cardinal sin of good English, but it is now accepted that there are many instances when a split infinitive is justified. In general, however, it is easy enough to avoid. Consider the following sentences:

(i) *She did not want to entirely surrender to his will.*
(ii) *He was instructed to discreetly talk to the Press.*

In both sentences there is no need for the split infinitive, for the adverb (*entirely, discreetly*) can be placed outside the infinitive without any change or injury to the sense:

(i) *She did not want to surrender entirely to his will.*
(ii) *He was instructed to talk to the Press discreetly.*
     or: *He was instructed to talk discreetly to the Press.*

When you can avoid the split infinitive without making the sentence unclear or ambiguous, then it is always preferable to do so. But there are times when the adverb can look clumsy or can change the meaning of the sentence if it does not separate the infinitive. Take the following example:

He was asked to discreetly drop a hint.

If *discreetly* were placed so that it did not split the infinitive, as it does above, then the sentence would read either *He was asked to drop a hint discreetly*, which sounds awkward and unnatural, or *He was discreetly asked to drop a hint*, which makes it unclear whether the person asking him is behaving in a discreet manner or whether *discreetly* refers to how the hint must be dropped. In this sentence the infinitive must be split if the right meaning is to be expressed clearly.

The easiest rule to remember about the split infinitive is to avoid it whenever there is no danger that the meaning will be ambiguous or awkwardly expressed as a result.

Words of similar form but different meaning

There are many pairs of words which sound almost the same (as distinct from homophones which sound identical, and which are dealt with in the next section). These similar-sounding words have quite different meanings, but sometimes they are close enough to one another to be confused even though their spelling or pronunciation should set them apart. In the following list, model sentences correctly illustrate each definition given.

accept: to take willingly
except: to leave out
  We accept your offer.
  My daughter excepted, all the family will be there.

adverse: unfavourable
averse: opposed
  Despite adverse conditions, the plane landed safely.
  He is clearly averse to my advice.

affect: to influence, to make a show of
effect: a result (*n.*), to bring about (*v.*)
  Does this change affect you?
  He affected complete indifference.
  What will be the effect of their decision?
  They will effect the new policy immediately.

allusion: a reference
illusion: a mistaken impression
  He made no allusion to his previous visit.
  He was under the illusion that he had visited me before.

alternate: every other
alternative: instead of
  The child hit every alternate lamp-post with his satchel.
  Bored with teaching, he chose farming as an alternative lifestyle.

amoral: with no understanding of good and evil
immoral: evil, especially sexually
  Children are amoral until they are taught by their parents.

He led an immoral life of crime and debauchery.

apposite: appropriate
opposite: facing
   It was not an apposite remark.
   The house is on the opposite side of the road.

appreciative: grateful
appreciable: enough to be noticed
   They were not appreciative of her hospitality.
   The difference will be appreciable.

beneficent: doing good
benevolent: kind, well-disposed
   He is the most beneficent supporter of the campaign.
   A generous donation does more than a benevolent heart.

beside: next to
besides: as well as
   He sat beside me in silence.
   There were several relations there besides the parents.

born: given birth to
borne: carried
   The baby was born in May.
   She had borne the baby for nine months.
   The raft was borne away by the strong current.

cache: a hidden store
cachet: prestige, exclusiveness
   The police found a cache of weapons in the basement.
   This expensive perfume has great cachet.

canvas: a kind of cloth
canvass: to ask for support
   She was carrying a canvas bag.
   Will you canvass for our parliamentary candidate?

censor: (*v.*) to delete matter regarded as offensive
censure: (*v.*) to criticize and rebuke severely
   Will you have to censor all the expletives in the play?
   I must censure that wholly unjustified accusation.

childish: like a child (*unattractive behaviour*)
childlike: like a child (*attractive qualities*)
  It was a very childish practical joke.
  There was a mysterious, childlike simplicity about him.

complacent: self-satisfied
complaisant: eager to please
  He had done little in his life to be complacent about.
  She was a complaisant girl, anxious to please.

complementary: balancing or completing
complimentary: expressing admiration
  They were complementary personalities – she was extrovert and he was
    quiet.
  They were very complimentary about my cooking.

contemptuous: full of contempt
contemptible: deserving contempt
  He is a proud, contemptuous man.
  It was a mean and contemptible trick.

continual (*of time*): repeated, frequently
continuous (*of place*): uninterrupted
  The meeting was prolonged by continual interruptions.
  The tanks around the palace formed a continuous line.

council: a governing body
counsel: advice/legal advisers
  The local council agreed to the scheme.
  He would not follow their counsel.
  Counsel warned that they would lose the case.

defective: faulty
deficient: insufficient
  This is a defective machine.
  There is a deficient supply of available goods.

definite: firm
definitive: complete and authoritative
  He at last gave us a definite answer.
  This is a definitive edition of the poet's complete works.

delusion: a false belief
illusion: a (deceptive) impression
  You must be suffering a terrible delusion if you think he's honest.
  The painting gives a wonderful illusion of space.

dependant: someone who depends on someone else
dependent: depending on
  He has four dependants: a wife and three children.
  His wife and three children are dependent on him.

disinterested: not prejudiced or personally involved
uninterested: not interested
  It was a disinterested argument, favouring neither side.
  The headmaster was clearly uninterested in my complaints.

deprecate: to disapprove of
depreciate: to lose value
  The environmentalists strongly deprecated the proposed development
    plan.
  Property will depreciate if the plan is implemented.

desert: a wasteland
dessert: the sweet part of a meal
  The landscape had been turned into a desert by the fire.
  Dessert is the last course of lunch or dinner.

distinct: clear
distinctive: clearly different
distinguished: admired for excellence
  His face betrayed distinct irritation.
  Each representative was wearing a distinctive uniform.
  She was a distinguished scientist.

efficient: businesslike
effectual: obtaining the desired result
effective: useful, practical
  She is an efficient administrator.
  Immediate and effectual action must be taken.
  Will this be an effective way of helping students?

eminent: universally admired
imminent: about to happen

Professor Lloyd is an eminent scholar.

Ths crisis is imminent; we cannot divert it any longer.

exceedingly: outstandingly
excessively: too much

It's an exceedingly good year for wine.

She felt excessively indignant at his views.

exhaust: to tire out
exhaustive: thorough, complete

Don't exhaust yourself.

The report gave an exhaustive account of the firm's achievements.

factious: turbulent
fractious: ready to quarrel

This factious behaviour will damage our reputation.

They were a difficult, fractious group of people to deal with.

factitious: created for a special purpose
fictitious: untrue

The documentary purported to be filming real lives, but it was clearly biased and factitious.

She gave a fictitious account of what he had done on the day of the crime.

flaunt: to show off
flout: to disregard

She flaunted her pink hair at the board meeting.

He flouted the law by drinking excessively, then driving home.

forbear: to refrain from
forebear: an ancestor

I will forbear from saying what I think until I calm down.

All the family's forebears had lived in the house.

gourmand: a greedy eater
gourmet: someone who knows about food and wine

The gourmand of the party ate twice as much as everyone else.

The gourmet of the party gave us a lecture on the wine.

hoard: to store; a treasure
horde: a multitude

A secret hoard of gold coins was found in the cellar.

Hordes of migratory tribes swept into Europe from Asia.

immigrant: someone who comes to live in another country
emigrant: someone who leaves his own country
Some immigrants would like to return to their native country.
Each year, thousands of emigrant Britons go abroad.

incredible: unbelievable
incredulous: unbelieving
I find your story incredible.
I told him the truth, but he remained incredulous.

infer: to gather
imply: to suggest
What do you infer from this discussion? What would you answer?
He was implying that I was wrong, but he would not speak openly.

ingenious: clever
ingenuous: frank, undeceiving
He devised an ingenious scheme to make his fortune.
The child's ingenuous remarks were very funny.

intelligent: naturally clever
intellectual: appealing to the power of the mind
He is an intelligent boy, but he lacks application.
He is an intellectual writer who confronts his reader with a myriad of
   ideas.

intense: strong, powerful
intensive: concentrated
The music was sombre and intense.
The students had to work hard, as the course was intensive.

inter: to bury
intern: to imprison
His body was interred last week.
The prisoners of war were interned in a secluded town.

insidious: cunningly harmful
invidious: offensive
It was an insidious attempt to jeopardize my career.
All his colleagues resented his invidious behaviour.

judicious: showing good judgement
judicial: relating to the law
    In this difficult situation, his answer was very judicious.
    A judicial body will be set up to resolve the inquiry.

licence: an official permit
license: to give official permission
    Please bring your driving licence with you.
    You will have to license this vehicle.

lightening: making or becoming lighter
lightning: a flash of light in the sky
    Slowly the dawn was lightening the sky.
    This tree was struck by lightning.

liqueur: a strong, sweet alcoholic drink
liquor: any liquid, especially alcoholic drink
    After dinner we had coffee and liqueurs.
    Young people cannot be served with liquor.

luxuriant: abundant
luxurious: expensively comfortable
    Everyone admired her luxuriant hair.
    Their luxurious bathroom had a marble bath.

masterful: dominating others
masterly: decisively skilful
    He was a proud and masterful man.
    It was a masterly stroke which won him the match.

metal: a hard substance
mettle: courageous spirit
    Gold is a heavy metal.
    This will put you on your mettle.

negligent: not careful enough
negligible: not worth noticing
    He was sacked because he was negligent in his duties.
    The difference between this shoe and that one is negligible.

notable: worthy of notice
notorious: famous for a bad reason

He made a notable point during the debate.
He was a notorious criminal.

observation: an act of watching/a remark
observance: formal behaviour
Observations are being made on where these rare birds nest.
He made the tactless observation that she looked older.
The traditional observances are always kept on this festival day.

official: formally authorized
officious: too eager to give orders or advice
It was an official occasion and all the children were smartly turned out.
His officious manner is irritating.

partly: not wholly
partially: to some extent
The machine is partly made of plastic.
She is partially blind.

perquisite: an additional benefit
prerequisite: a prior condition
If you join our firm you will enjoy many perquisites.
One prerequisite is that you must pass a medical examination.

personal: to do with oneself
personnel: staff
I must resign for personal reasons.
The personnel manager will interview candidates for the job.

practicable: that can be achieved
practical: efficient, down-to-earth
With a practicable solution, we can act immediately.
She was a practical, able girl.

practice: regular performance while learning
practise: to perform regularly while learning
Playing the piano well requires a lot of practice.
I will practise the piano for an hour a day.

precipitate: too hasty
precipitous: steep and dangerous
Our precipitate decision had serious consequences.

There are many precipitous slopes on this hill walk.

pre-empt: to take advantage of first
prevent: to stop from
He pre-empted what I was going to say by putting forward the proposal I was going to make.
A violent thunderstorm prevented me from leaving.

primary: first
primitive: raw; rough and ready
Our son attends the local primary school.
The primitive emotion in the painting was extraordinary.

principal: the head (*n.*)/chief (*adj.*)
principle: an underlying idea
The principal of the college is Dr Jenkins.
He told us his principal reason for resigning.
The principle is good, but will it work in practice?

prophecy: a foretelling of the future
prophesy: to foretell the future
The newspaper gave another gloomy economic prophecy.
Did you prophesy that this would happen?

proscribe: to ban
prescribe: to recommend
This organization is proscribed in our country; it has to operate secretly.
The doctor prescribed fresh air and early nights as the best cure.

punctual: on time
punctilious: attentive to detail
He was always punctual for appointments.
The secretary recorded the minutes of the meeting with punctilious care.

recourse: the hope of help
resort: to adopt a course of action
resource: a source of wealth or power
We do have recourse to Uncle John, who might help us pay off the debt.
Must you resort to such tricks so that you can get your own way?
North Sea Oil is a natural resource which is going to run out.

sanction: a restrictive action (*n.*)/to approve (*v.*)
sanctimonious: hypocritically holy
  We must impose sanctions on this repressive country.
  The school governors sanctioned the reinstatement of corporal
  punishment.
  His sanctimonious visits to her grave did not make up for the fact that
  he had never loved her.

seasonable: appropriate for the season
seasonal: varying with the seasons
  This is seasonable weather for January, which is usually the coldest month
  of the year.
  Vegetable prices vary according to seasonal changes.

stationary: not moving
stationery: writing materials
  Do not drive too close to stationary vehicles.
  Will you order some more stationery?

summon: to call formally
summons: a legal command
  I will summon him to my office.
  The court sent him a summons to appear the following week.

swat: to hit an insect
swot: to study hard
  He swatted the fly with his newspaper.
  He swotted all summer for his exams, but failed every one.

titillate: to arouse pleasantly
titivate: to make oneself look nice
  All pornography is intended to titillate.
  She went to the mirror to titivate herself.

tortuous: twisting, indirect
torturous: causing great pain
  It was a tortuous road through the mountain pass.
  The film was full of torturous scenes which were very disturbing.

track: a visible mark left by movement
tract: a large expanse
  Can you see the tracks the hares have made in the snow?

Our tract of land stretches from the river to those distant trees.

turbid: muddy, swollen
turgid: inflated, pompous
> The river was swollen and turbid after days of rain.
> It was a turgid speech, delivered in a pompous voice.

vindicate: to prove blameless
vindictive: spiteful
> We must vindicate your reputation, as the allegations against you are obviously false.
> He was a vindictive man who always bore grudges.

venal: for sale, corruptible
venial: pardonable
> He was an impressionable, venal boy who soon turned to crime.
> This is a venial offence, so you won't be punished this time.

Homophones

Homophones are words which sound identical but are spelt differently and have different meanings. For example, *hair* and *hare* sound just the same, but their meanings are totally different. Homophones cause most confusion over spelling: *He is over their* should read *He is over there.*

Here are some of the most common homophones:

aisle/isle
aloud/allowed
ascent/assent
beach/beech
board/bored
boy/buoy
canon/cannon
cereal/serial
chord/cord
coarse/course
cymbal/symbol
draft/draught
formally/formerly
gage/gauge
hair/hare
hall/haul
heir/air
hoard/horde
hole/whole
isle/aisle
its/it's
kernel/colonel
leak/leek
lessen/lesson
maize/maze
mare/mayor
mews/muse
moor/more
pail/pale
pause/paws

peer/pier
plain/plane
populace/populous
practice/practise
principal/principle
rain/reign/rein
raise/raze
right/rite
role/roll
sauce/source
serial/cereal
sew/sow
sight/site
son/sun
stair/stare
stake/steak
stationary/stationery
swat/swot
symbol/cymbal
tail/tale
their/there
to/too/two
vain/vane/vein
waist/waste
waive/wave
weather/whether
wholly/holy
who's/whose
yoke/yolk

Spelling rules

There are certain rules governing the spelling of groups of words, which should be adhered to if you want to improve your English. There may be a school of thought which holds that – if your writing is worth reading – it doesn't really matter about correct spelling; this is all very well if you turn out to be another George Bernard Shaw or James Joyce. Disregard the conventions, and you could be at a disadvantage when your errors are noticed. What is more, it could lead you into sloppy ways with the rest of your written and spoken English.

As the following guidelines show, English spelling is a minefield of inconsistencies. However, pay attention to these rules and you shouldn't go far wrong.

1. Doubling the final consonant

Words which end in a single consonant preceded by a single vowel, and which are accented on the last syllable, double their final consonant when a suffix (or ending) such as *-ing, -ed, -en, -er* or *-est* is added:

begin	→	*beginning, beginner*
enrol	→	*enrolling, enrolled* (but note: *enrolment*)
occur	→	*occurring, occurred, occurrence*
refer	→	*referring, referred* (but note: *reference*)

This same rule applies to one-syllable words when the final consonant is preceded by a single vowel:

sad	→	*sadden, sadder, saddest*
sin	→	*sinning, sinned, sinner*
sit	→	*sitting, sitter*

An exception is *bus* → *busing, bused;* horrible as these words are, they are now current vocabulary, and it should be remembered that bus is an abbreviation of *omnibus* (where the stress is on the first, not the last syllable).

2. Final -l

In words ending with *-l*, this is always doubled when the suffix is added:

model	→	*modelling,* etc.
propel	→	*propelling,* etc.
travel	→	*travelling,* etc.

Notice that this rule applies regardless of whether the stress falls on the last syllable or not (but in American English the accented first syllable gives *modeling, traveling,* whereas *propel* is stressed on the last and gives *propelling*).

3. Final -s

This is a problem; you will see *focus* → *focusing/focussing, focused/focussed; bias* → *biasing/biassing, biased/biassed.* It is one of the many inconsistencies of English – take your choice, but try to be consistent.

4. Two vowels before final consonant

If (unlike 1 above) **two** vowels precede the final consonant, then this last consonant is not doubled:

head	→	*heading,* etc.
conceal	→	*concealing,* etc.

Notice that *conceal* is also an exception to rule 2 above.

5. Final consonant not doubled

When the vowel preceding the last consonant is not stressed (compare rule 1), the last consonant is not doubled:

benefit	→	*benefiting,* etc.
cosset	→	*cosseting,* etc.
credit	→	*crediting,* etc.
debit	→	*debiting,* etc.
offer	→	*offering,* etc.
proffer	→	*proffering,* etc.

An exception to this rule is *worship* → *worshipping, worshipped,* etc.

6. Final -e

The rule here is that you drop a silent final *-e* before adding an ending beginning with a vowel:

advise	→	*advising, advisable*
love	→	*loving, lovable*

But if the word ends in *-ce* or *-ge*, you keep the *-e* when adding *-ous* or *-able*:

change	→	*changing,* but *changeable*
notice	→	*noticing,* but *noticeable*

If the added ending begins with a consonant, then retain the *-e*:

care	→	*careful, careless*
love	→	*lovelorn, lovely*

7. -ei- or -ie-?

(a) The old rule is 'i before e except after c'; what many forget is that this applies only when the *-ei-* or *-ie-* sounds like 'ee', as in *meet*:

ceiling, conceit, conceive, deceit, deceive, perceive, receipt, receive.

achieve, believe, brief, field, hygiene, niece, pierce, yield.

Exceptions to the rule are: *prima facie, species* (*-ie-* not *-ei-* despite the existence of a *c*) and *protein, seize, seizure, weir, weird.*

There are other words, in which the sound of the *-ei-* has shifted towards 'ee' from whatever was once considered correct, that could now be called exceptions: *caffeine, codeine, counterfeit, plebeian* are some examples. *Either* and *neither* should properly be pronounced 'eye-ther', 'nye-ther'.

(b) For sounds other than 'ee', the spelling is usually *-ei-*:

beige, height, leisure, neighbour, reign, skein, weight.

Exceptions to this include *friend, review, view.*

8. -ceed, -cede or -sede?

This is a much easier question to answer! Nearly all words ending in this sound are spelt -cede, so remember those that are not:

exceed, proceed, succeed, supersede.

9. fore- or for-?

Think about the word you want to spell: if the prefix suggests 'be*fore*hand' or 'in front of', then use *fore-* (*forebear* = ancestor, *forego* = precede). If the prefix suggests 'away', 'against', or implies exhaustion, prohibition or destruction, use *for-* (*forbear* = refrain, *forgo* = abstain from). Numerous words in this category are found to be spelt either way in the larger dictionaries.

10. -ful or -full?

When *-full* is added to a word, you change it to *-ful: cheerful, hopeful, successful,* etc. There's no change if you make a further addition of *-ly* (*cheerfully*) but notice *cheerfulness,* etc.

11. Words ending in -y

When a word ends in a consonant followed by a *-y,* change the *-y* to *-i-* before the suffixes *-ed, -er, -ies* and others:

carry	→	*carried, carrier, carries*
dry	→	*dried, drier, dries*
early	→	*earlier, earliest*
rely	→	*relied, relies, reliable, reliant*
study	→	*studied, studies*

The final *-y* does not change to *-i-* if it follows a vowel, or if the suffix begins with *i-*:

buy	→	*buyer, buying*
monkey	→	*monkeys*
say	→	*sayings, says* (but note: *said*)
study	→	*studying*

12. Plurals

(a) Most nouns form their plurals by adding -s. But if the singular form ends in -s, -ss, -x, -ch, -sh, -z or -zz you must add -es for the plural:

gas/gases, pass/passes, fox/foxes, church/churches, wish/wishes, fez/fezzes, buzz/buzzes.

Note that the -ch- sound is sibilant. When guttural (as in *loch*) or nearly so (*stomach*), the normal plural formation is found (*lochs* and *stomachs*). Note also that while *fez* usually doubles the -z, it can be written *fezes*; *quiz* always becomes *quizzes*.

(b) Nouns ending in -o are subject to several conditions in the formation of their plural forms. Quite a number add -es:

cargo/cargoes, echo/echoes, halo/haloes, potato/potatoes.

The rest simply add -s to the singular. It may help to remember that this group includes any where the -o is preceded by another vowel or -y- (*cuckoo/cuckoos, embryo/embryos*) or where the noun is an abbreviation (*kilo/kilos, rhino/rhinos*).

(c) When a singular noun ends in -y preceded by a consonant, the plural is usually formed by changing -y to -ie- before adding -s:

berry/berries, diary/diaries.

If the -y is preceded by a vowel, then the normal -s ending forms the plural:

day/days, donkey/donkeys.

(d) Nouns ending in -f or -fe usually must have the ending changed to -v before -es is added:

calf/calves, elf/elves, knife/knives, life/lives.

The exceptions to this rule simply add -s to the unaltered singular:

belief/beliefs, chief/chiefs, grief/griefs, gulf/gulfs, reef/reefs, roof/roofs.

And there are a very few that have either form:

hoof/hoof or hooves, scarf/scarfs or scarves.

Do not imagine that the foregoing guidelines cover all aspects of English spelling. They do not – and there are plenty more detailed chapters on the subject in other books. Refer to those if you need to. A list of 'difficult' words follows in our next section.

Difficult spellings

The following words cause spelling difficulties:

absence
abyss
accelerate
acceptable
access
accidentally
accommodation
achievement
acknowledgment/acknowledgement
acquaintance
acquiesce
advisable
aerial
ageing
aisle
alleged
allergic
anoint
appalling
applause
archaeology
assassination
athlete
autumnal
auxiliary
awkward

balk, baulk (verb)
balmy
believing
benefited
bicycle
blancmange
blond (of a man or his hair)
blonde (of a woman or her hair)
brochure

bulletin
bureau

camellia
campaign
carburettor
carcass/carcase
carefully
carriage
carrot
cease
cemetery
ceremony
chancellor
changeable
chaos
chaperon
chasm
clientele
colleague
coloration
column
commit(ment)
committee
concede
concession
conjuror
conqueror
conscience
conscientious
contemporary
contiguous
correspondence
corroborate
courtesy
curtsy

czar/tsar

dearth
debonair
deficient
descendant
desiccated
desperate

despise
diaphragm
dilapidate
diphtheria
diphthong
disappeared
disappointment
discrete
dissatisfied

ecstasy
eighth
eligible
enforceable
equivalent
erroneous
especially
exceed
excerpt
excessive
exhaustive
extraordinary
extremely

feasible
February
fiery
flu (not 'flu)
foible
forbade
forcible
forgo
forgotten
fulfil

gauge

geyser
goal
gorgeous
government
graffiti
grievance
guerilla/guerrilla

hallelujah
headache
heterogeneous
homogeneous
humorist
humorous
humour
hungry
hurrah/hurray
hyphen

icon/ikon
idyll
illegible
illiterate
immediately
imminent
impresario
inaugurate
independent
innocuous
inoculate
instil
install
instalment
inure
investor
irrelevant
isthmus

journey
judgment/judgement

khaki
knack
knowledge

knowledgeable
kowtow

laboratory
lacquer
languor
legible
liaison
lieutenant
lightning
liqueur
liquor
liquorice

manageable
manoeuvrable
marshal (noun and verb)
medieval
miniature
mischievous
mortgage
moustache

naive
necessary
negligible

obsolete
occasionally
occurred
offered
omitted
ophthalmic
opportunity
overrate

paediatric
pamphlet
parallel
parliament
persistent
persuade
possessive
precedent

predominant(ly)
prodigious
proffer
profited
pronunciation
psalm
pupillage
pursue

querulous
questionnaire

receptacle
referee
reminiscence
restaurateur
rhetoric

sacrilegious
salutary
schedule
secondary
secrecy
secretary
separate
sergeant
serviceable
silhouette
skilful
soliloquy
sovereignty
spontaneity
subsidiary
subtle
supersede
supplement
surveillance
swap

targeted
teetotaller
threshold
timorous
tonsillitis

tragedy
tunnelling
turquoise
twelfth

unconscionable

vaccination
vague
veneer
vigorous
vigour

visor

whooping cough
wisp
wisteria
withhold
wrath
wrestle

yield

zephyr

Always spell these words with s, not z:

advertise
advise
analyse
apprise

chastise
circumcise
comprise
compromise

demise
despise
devise
disguise

enterprise
excise

exercise

franchise

improvise
incise

merchandise

paralyse
prise

revise

supervise
surmise
surprise

televise

Prepositions

People do not always use the right prepositions after verbs, pronouns and adjectives. Below is a list of the most common words which take prepositions.

abhorrence *of*
abound *with*
absolve *from*
abundant *with/on*
accord *with*
acquiesce *in*
acquit *of*
adapted *for* (by nature)
adapted *to* (purpose)
admit *of*
affinity *between*
afflict *with*
agree *on* (a matter or point)
agree *to* (a proposal)
agree *with* (a person, statement, opinion)
aggravate *by*
alien *to*
amenable *to*
averse *to/from*

bestow *upon*
bored *with* or *by* (not *of*)

change *for* (a thing)
change *with* (a person)
chary *of*
cognizant *of*
compare *to* (to show similarities)
compare *with* (to note points of difference)
compatible *with*
comply *with*
confer *on* (to bestow *upon*)
confer *with*
confide *in* (trust *in*)
confide *to* (entrust *to*)

conform *to*
in conformity *with*
congratulate *on*
connive *at*
consequent *upon*
convenient *for* (purpose)
convenient *to* (person)
conversant *with*
correspond *to* (a thing)
correspond *with* (a person)

deficient *in*
derogatory *to*
die *for* (a cause)
die *of* (an illness)
differ *from* (be different)
differ *with* (disagree)
different *from*
disappointed *of* (what we cannot have)
disappointed *in* (what we have)
dissent *from* (not *to*)
distaste *for*

essential *to*
exception *to* (a rule, statement)
exempt *from*

glad *at* (a piece of news)
glad *of* (a possession)
guiltless *of*

identical *with*
impatient *of* (things)
impatient *with* (persons)
impervious *to*
incidental *to*
inculcate *upon* someone (not: inculcate *with*)
independent *of*
indicative *of*
ineligible *for*
inflict *upon*
influence *over/with* (a person)
influence *on/upon/in* (persons or things)
infuse *into* (someone)

inspired *by*
instil *into*
involve *in*
irrespective *of*

martyr *for* (a cause)
martyr *to* (a disease, etc.)

negligent *of* (noun)

oblivious *of* (not *to*)

part *from* (persons)
part *with* (things)
preferable *to*
prevail *against* (things)
prevail *upon* (persons)
profuse *in*
profusion *of*

reconcile *to* (thing)
reconcile *with* (person)
regard *as*
relevant *to*
responsible *for* (something)
responsible *to* (someone)

satisfied *of* (fact)
satisfied *with* (things)
sensitive *to*
susceptible *to*

taste *for* (art, etc.)
taste *of* (food)
thirst *for/after* (knowledge)

unconscious *of* (not *to*)

You can ignore the supposed rule that a sentence should not end with a preposition. The fact that many sentences and clauses naturally end in this way has always been a feature of English. Often, the preposition <u>needs</u> to go at the end: *He is the best person I can think of* could not be rephrased *He is the best person of whom I can think,* nor could *What are you waiting for?* be rephrased *For what are you waiting?*

Some prepositions cannot go at the end: *During which month wil you be away?* could not be rewritten *Which month will you be away during?*

When a sentence has a relative clause, then the preposition may stand either before the relative pronoun or at the end of the clause:

The quandary in which we find ourselves is very awkward.
Or: *The quandary which we find ourselves in is very awkward.*

If you have a choice as to where the preposition can go, choose whatever sounds most natural.

A and *an*

A and *an* are indefinite articles. Unlike the definite article (*the*) they refer to someone or something whose precise identity is not specified. Although they are among the most common words in the language, doubt sometimes arises as to which should be used.

A is used:

(a) before all consonants: *a man, a tree, a book.*
(b) before an aspirated h: *a horse, a hero, a humorist.*
(c) before the letter u when sounded like 'you': *a unit, a use, a union.*
(d) before the diphthong eu: *a European, a eulogy.*
(e) before the letter o in *one* and *once.*
(f) before words beginning with y: *a year, a yellow dress, a youth.*

An is used:

(a) before a vowel sound: *an animal, an example, an ignorant woman, an orange, an umbrella.*
(b) before a mute h: *an hour, an honest man.*

The pronunciation of *hotel,* and of *history* with its derivatives, has changed. It used to be considered correct to say *an 'otel, an 'istory, an 'istorian, an 'istorical novel,* with the h silent; this now sounds old-fashioned, and you should sound the h (*a hotel, a history,* etc.). Somewhat longer ago, people spoke of *an humorist* (mute h) – and in the Bible we read that *Esau was an hairy man.* Times change!

Hyphens

It is easy to become confused over the proper use of hyphens. The main purpose of a hyphen is to join two (or more) words together, making them a single compound word with its own meaning:

an *ex-President* is a former President;
a *co-director* works with other directors.

The absence of a hyphen can lead to misunderstanding:

I must re-cover the sofa (with new material).
I must recover the sofa (from the person I lent it to).

Swimming is excellent recreation (exercise).
The film's re-creation of the 1950s was very convincing (background, dress, etc.).

After his time in prison, he was a reformed character (no longer a criminal).
They re-formed the society and met once a week (started up again).

Prefixes like *co-* and *pre-* should have a hyphen when the next part of the word begins with the same vowel: *co-ordinate, pre-empt.* This rule does not apply in American English.

Hyphens can contribute considerably to clarity: *You must read two hundred odd pages a day* reads strangely, so write *You must read two hundred-odd pages a day.*

Similarly, *An eighteenth-century writer* is more elegant than *A writer who wrote in the eighteenth century* – which is the long way of expressing it.

There are several word combinations which are hyphenated when they come before a noun, but not when they come after:

He is a well-known author.
But: *This author is well known.*

She is a part-time worker.
But: *She works part time.*

This is an out-of-date system.
But: *This system is out of date.*

Distinctions such as these cause frequent mistakes.

You should never hyphenate in adverb + adjective combinations: *a newly married couple.* Also remember that *no one* is always written as two words.

Anyone/any one; everyone/every one: There is a simple rule on when to use these as two words and when they should be written as one.

When you are talking of separate things or people, use two words:

Any one of the two will do.
We like all the poems; every one deserves to win.

When you are talking generally, use one:

Anyone can compete.
Everyone will be there.

Abbreviations

Many written abbreviations are shown by a full stop at the end (for example, *10 a.m., Capt. Lloyd-Jones, Please read p. 8*), while others do not have a full stop. First, consider the two groups below:

1. No full stop

Abbreviations which end with the same letter as the word spelt out in full should not take a full stop – *Dr* does not need one, because both *Dr* and *Doctor* end in r. Other examples are:

cwt	(hundredweight)
Ltd	(Limited)
Mr	(Mister)
Mrs	(Missis, originally Mistress)
Ms	(pronounced 'miz' but stands for Mrs or Miss)
Revd	(Reverend – not to be written Rev'd)
St	(street or Saint)

2. With full stop

Abbreviations which do *not* end in the same letter as the unshortened form need a full stop:

anon.	(anonymous)
c.o.d.	(or *C.O.D.* cash on delivery)
e.g.	(for example – from the Latin *exempli gratia*)
etc.	(and the rest – Latin *et cetera*)
i.e.	(that is – Latin *id est*)
Jan.	(January – other months are shortened in the same way)
Mon.	(Monday – other days are similarly abbreviated)
MS.	(manuscript – the plural is MSS.)
p.	(page or penny/pence)
P.L.C.	(Public Limited Company)
P.S.	(postscript – Latin *post scriptum*)
R.S.V.P.	(please reply – French *répondez s'il vous plaît*)
tv.	(or *TV,* television)

Although there may be some disagreement as to whether or not *penny/pence* should have a full stop when abbreviated in writing, it is always better to

<u>say</u> 'one penny', 'two pence', 'ten pence' and so on. Don't say 'pee'. Also avoid saying 'I saw it on tee-vee' and 'At the end of Jan or early Feb', however much you may hear these. Words such as *page, manuscript* and *et cetera* are never spoken of in their abbreviated forms.

Now look at some of the exceptions to the rule in group 2 above:

(a) Words whose short form has become more common than their original do not need a full stop:

bra (brassière)
bus (omnibus)
exam (examination)
flu (influenza)
fridge (refrigerator)
phone (telephone)
plane (aeroplane)
pub (public house)
rep (repertory theatre)
vet (veterinary surgeon)
zoo (zoological garden)

(b) Colloquial abbreviations – which in time might join those in (a) above, whether we like it or not – do not need a full stop:

co-op (co-operative)
demo (demonstration)
recap (recapitulation)
telly (television)
trad (traditional)
vac (vacation)

(c) No full stops for numerical abbreviations (*1st, 2nd, 3rd,* etc.)

3. Full stop optional

Words shortened to a sequence of initials do not usually have full stops if they stand for companies, countries, organizations or qualifications which are generally spoken of by those initials. This is preferable. However, it is quite all right to place full stops in these abbreviations; frequently the choice is according to a long-established 'house' style favoured by the printer or company concerned. For example:

BBC or *B.B.C.* (British Broadcasting Corporation)
PO or *P.O.* (Post Office)
USA or *U.S.A.* (United States of America)
NATO or *N.A.T.O.* (North Atlantic Treaty Organization)
QC or *Q.C.* (Queen's Counsel)

In some cases the initials have become accepted acronyms (*Nato, Unesco, Naafi*, etc.) but are not always printed as such. Another instance where inconsistency rules is the abbreviation for Public Limited Company; *P.L.C.* is correct, but you will see *PLC, P.l.c., Plc*, and *plc* dotted around various letterheads (according to the designer's instructions) and then carried down into the small print – quite unreasonably.

Punctuation

Without punctuation, reading would be slow and difficult. Full stops, commas and the other tools of punctuation do to the written language what pauses, intonation and gesture do to speech. A correctly punctuated piece of writing takes much less effort to read than one where you have to supply the stops, commas, etc., yourself.

Comma

Commas are either used unnecessarily or not enough. The comma marks the shortest pause in the sentence and, when used correctly, has several uses:

(a) To replace *and* in separating a series of words belonging to the same part of speech, whether nouns, adjectives, verbs or adverbs:

I saw Angela, Sarah and Clare.
The car slowed down, stalled and stopped.
He made conversation cheerfully, wittily and interestingly.
He was an extrovert, restless and ambitious man.

The word before *and* takes a comma only in certain instances, for example:

Her favourite shops were Selfridges, John Lewis, and Marks and Spencer.

Without the comma after *John Lewis* it might appear that *Marks and Spencer* were two different shops.

(b) To separate words when a person is addressed:

Will you, when you have time, please write to him.

To separate words and phrases in apposition and participial phrases:

Henry the Eighth, King of England, had six wives.
Having looked at the menu, I chose fish soup.
All things considered, I prefer to stay at home.

(c) In complex sentences, where a short pause is required to separate clauses:

Unless you change your ways, you must go.
This man, who always bought property in the most exclusive areas, was a millionaire.

A comma would not, however, be needed if the above sentence read:

This man who bought the property was a millionaire.

In this sentence the adjective clause *who bought the house* defines the subject of the sentence: the man is identified as the one who bought the house. When the adjective clause in a sentence defines the subject, no comma is needed. When the adjective clause merely <u>comments</u> on the subject without affecting its definition, then commas are required to separate the clause from the main subject and the verb. Thus in the sentence above, *This man, who always bought property in the most exclusive areas, was a millionaire,* the adjective clause comments on the subject, giving additional information about the man, but does not identify him, as in *This man who bought the property* .... When the adjective clause is a non-defining one, commas are necessary.

(d) To separate two parts in double sentences, when the second subject is expressed:

He wanted to argue, but the teacher would not allow him.

If the subject of the two parts is the same, then no comma should be used:

He wanted to argue but was afraid of getting into trouble.

Commas are usually unnecessary with words like *therefore, however, at last,* etc., except for emphasis:

Every student must therefore revise thoroughly.

This sentence would be made more emphatic if a comma was put after *must* and *therefore*:

Every student must, therefore, revise thoroughly.

Unless you wish to stress the meaning, it is better to omit commas when using *however, therefore* and similar words.

Full stop

The full stop indicates the end of a sentence:

While making the choice of life, you neglect to live.

There are few mistakes to be made over full stops. Remember that they are an effective and straightforward means of ending a sentence, but should not be used exclusively. If they are not used in conjunction with other punctuation marks, the effect tends to look rather childish and stilted, as in:

Please call me in the morning. I have something important to discuss. I shall be in the office by nine. It will not take longer than five minutes.

This would obviously read better as:

Please call me in the morning, as I have something important to discuss. I shall be in the office by nine and it will not take longer than five minutes.

Question and exclamation marks do not take full stops after them.

Semicolon

The semicolon marks a longer pause than a comma, but a shorter one than a full stop. It is often useful when separating two sentences which could stand independently but are closely connected in sense:

Paul caught the earliest train the following morning; he was anxious to arrive as early as he could.

It can also be used effectively to emphasize the contrast between two sentences:

Every wise man doubts; and every fool is certain.

The right use of the semicolon before conjunctions marking an extra pause between two sentences (*and, but, yet, or,* etc.) should be contrasted with their incorrect use with conjunctions that make the subordinate clause dependent on the main clause (*if, when, though,* etc.). The semicolon should never be used with these:

He will be ready to overlook the mistake; when you have apologized.
She must wonder what the trouble is; if you leave without any explanation.

In the first example the semicolon should be replaced by a comma and in the second by a dash, or by recasting the sentence:

If you leave without any explanation, she will wonder what the trouble is.

The semicolon is also used to divide the items introduced by a sentence followed by a colon:

There were many things to notice about this extraordinary palace: the delicate plasterwork on the walls; the elegant porticoes in the courtyards; and the pools and fountains that were everywhere.

If you are uncertain about the semicolon, avoid it; but it can be a very effective punctuation mark.

Colon

The colon, indicating a fuller pause than a semicolon, is now used almost exclusively to precede lists, summaries or quotations:

The doctor noted various symptoms: high blood pressure, migraine and nausea.
He briefly summarized the main issues: the cost of restoring the town hall; the need for controlling traffic in the town centre; the programme for the summer music festival; and the latest visit to the twin town.

The colon is often used after expressions such as *to sum up, for example, namely, to resume, the following,* etc.

The colon can also be used to separate two sentences in order to emphasize the contrast between them, or to place a breathing space between them. This use is similar to that of the semicolon, and the semicolon is now the more common and acceptable punctuation mark for separating clauses. The colon may still be used in this way:

Man proposes: God disposes.

Question mark

The question mark is used after a direct question:

Is she sincere?

It is never used after an indirect question:

He asked whether she was sincere.

The question mark must not be used in place of a derogatory comment:

The headmaster tried to explain his irrational behaviour by saying he had been worried by family (?) troubles.

There are better ways of being frank or ironic.

Exclamation mark

Exclamation marks should be confined to true exclamations, e.g.

Help!
Long live the king!

They may also be used with an exclamatory *how* or *what:*

How fit you look!
What a piece of work is man!

Sometimes an exclamation mark is appropriate at the end of a sentence to convey the feeling or tone behind it:

She even went as far as to write to the bishop to complain!

Avoid excessive use of the exclamation mark. Well-chosen words can speak for themselves and do not need pointers to indicate their tone.

Brackets

Brackets are used to enclose a parenthesis – an explanation or interpolation – in a sentence. They should be reserved for explanations and interpolations which are genuinely independent of the grammar and sense of the rest of the sentence:

The experiment described (see pages 6–10) is a real innovation.

Punctuation marks should always be placed outside the closing bracket if they belong to the main sentence and not to the parenthesis:

The experiment described is a real innovation (see pages 6–10).

If the opening bracket introduces a new and complete sentence, then the punctuation goes inside the closing bracket:

Mrs Lloyd opened the door. (By now I was quivering with nerves and had forgotten all the pleasant chat that I had carefully rehearsed.)

Occasionally punctuation marks are placed inside the closing bracket of a parenthesis which is inserted at the end or in the middle of the main sentence. In this case the punctuation does properly belong to the parenthesis and not to the main sentence:

I walked into the garden (how unchanged it was!) and waited for her.

Dash

The dash tends to be overused by lazy writers who forget that other punctuation marks are often more appropriate. It should not supplant commas, colons, brackets, etc.

The double dash can be used for parenthesis, like brackets, to introduce an explanation or additional information that is grammatically independent of the main sentence. When used in this way the dash suggests a more vigorous, abrupt tone than brackets:

The director announced – as the staff suspected – that the firm was going into liquidation.

A single dash introduces an explanation or amplification of what immediately precedes it:

They had brought fresh bread, cheese, pâté and wine – all the ingredients for a successful French picnic.

In the following examples the dash has been misused:

The expectant crowd – packed together under a merciless August sun which was beating down on the stadium, and making the presence of others unbearable – was chanting for the arrival of the favourite.

The subject of the sentence, *the expectant crowd,* is lost in the long and involved parenthesis. The dashes should be replaced by commas.

Anne – the pupil in disgrace – was not repentant.

Words and phrases in apposition to proper names should always be placed between commas, not dashes.

Quotation marks

Quotation marks denote direct speech and may be single or double, though single are preferable. A quotation within direct speech indicated by single quotation marks should be enclosed by double quotation marks, and vice versa:

'Let me refer you,' advised the lecturer, 'to the chapter entitled "Dionysus and the Ancient Greeks".'

Quotation marks are also used to denote titles of articles in magazines, songs and chapters of books. They should not be used for the titles of books of the Bible. Quotation marks to indicate slang or technical words and phrases, or for words used in an unusual sense, should be used sparingly. They should never be used as a substitute for finding the best word.

It is not difficult to distinguish direct and indirect speech, yet the following error is not uncommon:

She was furious when he referred to her as 'one of his least successful candidates'.

This is an indirect statement; if it was a direct statement then the person making the comment would refer to *'one of my least successful candidates'.* Quotations should be used only to signify direct speech, not indirect speech or reported speech as in the following:

She said that although she 'was sorry that her dog had bitten Mrs Smith's daughter, the child should not have alarmed the animal by climbing through the kitchen window.'

*She said **that*** introduces a reported statement. *She said, 'I am sorry that my dog, etc.'* would indicate direct speech.

When direct speech is interrupted by words such as *he said,* then the punctuation marks go **outside** the quotation marks if they do not naturally form part of the utterance if uninterrupted:

'I am anxious', he said, 'that we face the facts.'

If the sentence was not interrupted by *he said* there would be no comma after *anxious*; the comma preceding *he said* therefore goes after the quotation mark. The full stop at the end of the sentence comes inside the quotation mark because it closes the quotation as well as the quotation marks. Compare with the following example:

'According to Father O'Grady, the local Catholic priest,' he said, 'more people are attending confession than in previous years.'

The comma after *priest* goes inside the quotation mark because there would be a comma in the sentence without the interruption of *he said.*

There is little agreement on whether commas should follow verbs of saying which introduce direct speech. Both *He said, 'Here she is.'* and *He said 'Here she is.'* are acceptable, though omitting the comma is preferable on the grounds that the sentence is less cluttered. Commas always follow verbs of saying which interrupt or follow direct speech.

Apostrophe

The apostrophe marks the omission of a letter in certain words, e.g. *don't* for *do not,* and *I'll* for *I will* or *shall.* These abbreviated forms should be avoided in formal writing.

The apostrophe also denotes the possessive, e.g. *the lady's gloves.* The possessive is formed by adding *'s* to the noun if it is singular and *s'* if it is plural, e.g. *the ladies' gloves.* If the singular noun ends in *s* and is a monosyllable then 's is added after it:

James's nose is very long.

If a singular noun ending in *s* has more than one syllable, the possessive is best indicated by 's (although *s'* is possible):

Thomas's car is red. (Possible: *Thomas' car is red.*)

The most usual errors over apostrophes occur when they are used with possessive pronouns (see p.127) and certain nouns which are made plural. Possessive nouns never take an apostrophe: *Is this yours? No, it's theirs.*

The plurals of certain words like *MPs, 1960s,* are often written *MP's, 1960's.* This is wrong. Remember that the apostrophe is used only to indicate certain abbreviations and the possessive, not the plural of nouns.

Capital letters

The first word of a sentence always begins with a capital letter. Capital letters are also used for:

(a) proper names like *Jane, Michael, Rome, India.* Two-word geographical names should take a capital letter for each word: *Mount Everest, River Derwent.*

(b) the days of the week and the months of the year.

(c) the first word in direct speech: *He said 'Run for your life!'*

(d) names of organizations and titles: *Lord Aberdale, Dr Heskith, the Department of Trade.*

(e) the first and other important words in the titles of books, plays, films, etc.: *The History of Rasselas, Kind Hearts and Coronets.*

Pronunciation

The pronunciation of English varies as much within the United Kingdom as it does throughout the world. Received pronunciation – the Queen's English – is no longer considered the best, although it is still considered the standard. Television and radio presenters, who all used to speak with a uniform southern English accent, now commonly speak with regional accents.

Received pronunciation still sets a valuable standard in speaking English and in many instances is preferable to the many other choices. Students learning English as a second language find it helpful to learn the standard pronunciation before the regional variations.

American English is gaining a stronger and stronger hold on English pronunciation. Let us resist this influence and keep our own distinctive way of speaking. Some of the stress patterns in American pronunciation sound ugly to the English ear, particularly the feature of stressing the third to last syllable in certain adverbs ending in -arily. Stressing the a in, for example, *temporarily* produces an unpleasant whine that is absent from the English pronunciation, which stresses the first syllable.

In the following selection of words which often are mispronounced or give cause for thought, any American variations are shown alongside their preferred (British English) pronunciation.

Antarctic, Arctic	do not drop the first c
anti-	rhymes with *scanty* (Am.: 'ant-eye')
apposite	stress the first syllable, as in *opposite*
arbitrarily	stress the first syllable
Argentine	rhymes with *line*
aristocrat	first syllable stressed (Am.: second syllable stressed)
asterisk	often wrongly said as 'asterix'
ate	rhymes with *let* (Am.: rhymes with *late*)
banal	stress the second a, as in *banana* (Am.: stress the first, like *anal*)
blackguard	pronounce 'blagg-ard'
bouquet	first syllable as in *book*, not *bow* (*and arrow*); stress the last syllable

breeches	rhymes with *witches*
brochure	stress the first syllable (although to stress the last is not wrong)
centenary	stress the second syllable (Am.: stress the first)
chimera	the ch sounds as k; the i-sound is best kept short; stress the second syllable
chiropodist	ch sounds as k, but 'sh' is acceptable; stress the second syllable
chiropractic(e)	ch sounds as k, never 'sh'; stress the first syllable
combat (noun & verb)	stress the first syllable (Am.: the last)
communal	stress the first syllable
commune (noun & verb)	stress the noun's first syllable, the verb's last
comparable	stress the first syllable, not the second
contrarily	stress the first syllable when meaning *on the contrary*, but the second when it = *perversely*
controversy	stress the first syllable
contribute	stress the second syllable
courteous	rhyme the first syllable with *curt*
deity	'dee-ity' not 'day-ity'
demesne	the second syllable rhymes with *mane*
deteriorate	don't drop the fourth syllable (i.e. not 'deteeri- ate')
dilemma	short i before stressed e, not 'dye²'
diphtheria	sound the ph as f, not as p
diphthong	sound the ph as f, not as p
disciplinary	stress the first syllable (but stress on the third is acceptable)
dour	rhymes with *floor*, not *flower*
dynasty	first syllable 'din' (Am.: 'dye')
economic	either 'eck-o' or 'ee-ko'
ego	correctly, 'eggo'; acceptable, 'ee-go'
egoism	'eggo²' not 'ee-go-' (Am.: usually 'ee-go-')
either	'eye-ther' or 'ee-ther' (Am.: 'ee-ther')
envelop	stress the second syllable
envelope	stress the first syllable, sounding it 'en' not 'on'
exquisite	stress the first syllable
February	do not omit the first r
forbade	rhyme the second syllable with *bad*
formidable	stress the first syllable

fracas	'frack-ah' is the singular, 'frack-ahz' is the plural (Am.: 'frake-us' for both)
garage	stress the first syllable; last rhymes with *camouflage* or *large*, not *ridge* (Am.: stress last)
genuine	the last syllable rhymes with *engine* (Am.: with *combine*)
harass(ment)	stress the first syllable, never the second
heinous	rhyme the first syllable (a diphthong) with *hay;* some authorities accept 'hee'
hospitable	stress the first syllable
idyll, idyllic	i as in *irritable*
inchoate	stress the second syllable, ch as k
insult (noun & verb)	stress the noun's first syllable, the verb's last
integral	stress the first syllable
invalid (noun & adj.)	stress the first syllable of the noun, the second syllable of the adjective
invalid (verb)	stress the third, rhyming with 'leed'
inventory	stress the first syllable
irrevocable	stress the second syllable
jewellery	pronounce 'jewel-ry', not 'jool-ery'
kilometre	stress the first syllable, as in *kilogram*
laboratory	stress the second syllable (Am.: stress the first, with further stress on 'tory')
lichen	like *liken*, but 'litchen' acceptable
lieutenant	first syllable as in *left*, but in British naval use almost drop the f (Am.: 'loo-')
mandatory	stress the first syllable
metallurgy	stress the second syllable (Am.: the first)
migraine	first syllable as in *me* (Am.: like *my*)
miscellany	stress the second syllable (Am.: first)
momentary, -ily	stress the first syllable
nascent	say 'nass-' not 'nace-'
necessarily	in careful speech, stress the first syllable
obligatory	stress the second syllable
participle	stress the first syllable; often 'part-ciple'
patron	rhymes with *matron* ('pay²')
patronize	first syllable like *pat*

porpoise	'por-puss' not 'por-poise'
primarily	stress the first, not the second syllable
privacy	preferably a short i, as in *privet* (Am.: long as in *private*)
process (noun & verb)	in both, stress the first syllable (but not when the verb = *to walk in processsion*)
pronunciation	second syllable as in *nun*, not *noun*
protest (noun & verb)	stress the first syllable in the noun, the last in the verb
quasi	first syllable as in *say*, last as in *eye*
rampage (noun & verb)	stress the noun's first syllable, the verb's last
really	rhymes with *dearly*, not *freely*
renaissance	stress the second syllable
renege	rhymes with *league*
research (noun & verb)	in both, stress the second syllable
Saudi	rhymes with *dowdy*, not *bawdy*
schedule	first syllable as in *shed* (Am.: 'sked')
sovereignty	pronounce as 'sov-renty'
strength	ng as in *hung*, not 'strenth'
suppose	avoid 'spose' in careful speech
surveillance	do not drop the l, say 'sur-vayl-lance'
temporarily	stress the first syllable, not third
transfer (noun & verb)	stress the noun's first syllable, the verb's last
transferable	stress the first syllable (but stress on the second is common and acceptable)
veterinary	stress the first syllable, and say 'vet-rin-ry'
voluntarily	stress the first syllable
yoghurt	pronounce 'yogg-hurt' (Am.: 'yoh-gurt')

Foreign words and phrases

In general, when you can find good English equivalents for the many foreign words and phrases that now have currency in English, use them. Foreign words are often used out of affectation or pretension but some can be used to good effect in describing states or feelings which do not have a direct English equivalent or could be put in English only very lengthily. For example, the everyday Latin term curriculum vitae would take many more words to describe in English.

The English are reluctant language-learners, and with the decline of Latin and Greek in education it is important to be familiar with foreign words and phrases that are now a valuable part of our language. Very often you will see these printed in italics, especially where they have not been fully absorbed into current English.

a fortiori
Latin for *from yet firmer ground* or *with stronger reason*. It is a term from logic and is used to introduce a fact that, if already accepted as true, must then be doubly true:

She could not have been cured in a month, a fortiori not in a day.

With the exception of very formal writing, it is better to find an English equivalent for this term.

agent provocateur (plural: agents provocateurs)
French for describing a person who is employed to lead others – by pretending to be an accomplice – into acts for which they will be discovered and punished:

Communist guerrillas have been arrested after being betrayed by *agents provocateurs* employed by the government.

al fresco (also often alfresco)
Italian for *in the open air*. It is used only to describe eating in the open air; you do not swim *al fresco* or go to an alfresco theatre:

One of the delights of an evening's opera at Glyndebourne is the *al fresco* dinner in that perfect garden setting.

alibi

Latin for *elsewhere*. In informal speech it has come to be used generally, but formally it is a legal term:

He denied being at the scene of the crime, giving as his alibi the fact that he was in hospital.

alma mater

Latin for *bounteous mother*. It is used by graduates to refer to the university where they studied.

amanuensis (plural: amanuenses)

Latin for someone who writes from dictation. The term is usually reserved to describe the personal and private secretary of an elderly individual:

As well as her housekeeper, Miss Armitage now employed an amanuensis – for her sight was fading and her fingers stiffening with arthritis.

ambience/ambiance

This is French for *surroundings* and is useful to describe a general atmosphere:

The club's ambience was dark and romantic.

amour propre

Means *self-love* or *self-esteem* in French:

A writer's *amour propre* is dependent on the success of his books.

aplomb

A useful French word for describing certain actions that are performed in a self-possessed and spirited way:

He played a difficult piece on the piano with great aplomb.

a priori

Latin for *from the previous*. To argue *a priori* is to argue from assumed premises, not from experience:

There is no *a priori* reason for our failure; we must have made some mistake.

à propos (also often apropos)

French for *with reference to*. Do not use it in formal writing.

Apropos (of) our conversation yesterday....

bête noire (plural: *bêtes noires*)

French for *black beast*. In English it is used to mean *pet hate* – something which a person particularly dislikes:

Our English teacher's *bête noire* was the split infinitive; he was always pointing them out.

billet-doux (plural: billets-doux)

French for *love letter*. It is usually used in a humorous sense:

He had hidden a billet-doux under her pillow.

blasé

French for *surfeited with pleasure* (and with the senses dulled as a result):

Living in Oxford had made him blasé about the beauties of the city.

bona fide

Latin for *good faith, genuine*. The adjectival use is the more proper, and to be preferred to a substantive form which is sometimes seen (*His bona fides* – i.e. his genuineness – *impressed us*):

As a bona fide unmarried mother, she got a council flat immediately.

bourgeois

Means *middle class* in French. It is commonly used in a deprecating sense:

He was everything a bourgeois stood for – concerned only for his respectability.

carte blanche (plural: cartes blanches)

French for a *white paper*, used to mean a *free hand* or *full permission:*

As the consultant brought in by the firm, she had carte blanche to suggest improvements.

chacun à son goût

Means in French *Each man to his taste:*

'So you like pigs' brains?' he asked. *'Chacun à son goût.'*

chargé d'affaires (plural: chargés d'affaires)

French for a person responsible for affairs of state abroad, often an acting ambassador:

We regret that there is no ambassador for Brazil at present, only a chargé d'affaires.

chez
French for *at the house of*. It always takes the name of a person or persons after it:

The party is *chez* Paul.

chic
A French word for smart, stylish clothes:

She looked very chic in her pink beret and blue suit.

contretemps (plural: contretemps)
French for a *misunderstanding*, an *awkward mishap*:

Arriving early led to the unfortunate contretemps of finding my hosts in the middle of an argument.

coup de foudre (plural: *coups de foudre*)
The literal French meaning is *thunderbolt*. This is used to describe a sudden and unexpected event or love at first sight:

It was a *coup de foudre* – they were married in two months.

coup de grâce (plural: *coups de grâce*)
French for *finishing stroke*:

I put the dying animal out of its pain by one swift *coup de grâce*.

curriculum vitae (plural: curricula vitae)
Latin for *an account of one's life*. It is often abbreviated to c.v., and is used only in job advertisements:

Applicants must send a full curriculum vitae.

de facto, de jure
In Latin, de facto means *in fact* or *in reality*. It is a legal term contrasting with the parallel phrase *de jure*. A de facto leader does not rule on a legal basis, but simply because he has won his position. He may gain official status later if he becomes a de jure ruler – if his position becomes legally regularized:

An army colonel, he overthrew the country's president and was its de facto leader until elections were held.

de rigueur
The literal French meaning is *of strictness*. In English it is used (often slightly humorously) to mean *required by convention or fashion*:

Miniskirts were *de rigueur* in the 1960s.

deus ex machina
Latin for *the god from the machine*. The term is taken from Greek drama, where a complicated plot would be resolved by the sudden appearance of a god. It can describe situations other than the plots of plays and films:

My aunt arrived, like a *deus ex machina,* and normality was miraculously restored.

dilettante (plural: dilettanti or dilettantes)
The Italian word for one who dabbles in the arts or sciences but does not pursue them seriously:

He played the piano in a dilettante fashion, never practising.

double entendre
French for the double meaning there might be in puns and innuendoes:

In the after-dinner speech he made many double entendres which set the guests laughing.

ennui
Describes a state of languor and boredom in French:

Ennui was a nineteenth-century disease among rich people who had nothing to do.

entente cordiale
French for a complete and cordial understanding between two sovereign powers:

An entente cordiale between France and Britain has meant that the Channel Tunnel will now go ahead.

esprit de corps
French for a spirit of solidarity and unity with one's peers:

The esprit de corps of the rebels gave them the courage to bring down the dictatorship.

ex officio
Latin for *by virtue of his office,* in general used only to describe the position of committee members:

As the secretary of the society he will be an ex officio member of all the subcommittees.

faux pas (plural: faux pas)

Means *false step* in French. It is usually used to describe tactless mistakes:

She made a terrible faux pas when she congratulated my mother on her success, which was supposed to be a secret.

graffiti

Italian for scribbling or drawings on walls:

The school walls were covered in graffiti.

hors de combat

Literally, in French, *out of the fight*. It is used to mean *injured* or in some way unable to do something:

I'm afraid I'm *hors de combat:* I've sprained my ankle and can't play tennis today.

infra dignitatem

Latin for *below one's dignity*. It is usually abbreviated in colloquial use to infra dig:

As a professional musician she considered it infra dig to play duets with her sister.

in loco parentis

Latin for *in the place of a parent*. A legal term defining the relationship of a principal to his pupils:

While his parents were abroad, the headmaster acted *in loco parentis*.

insouciance

French for *unconcern, carelessness:*

His insouciance about the risks he was taking was remarkable.

jeu d'esprit

Means *witticism* in French:

He greeted my late arrival with a sardonic *jeu d'esprit*.

kudos

A Greek word meaning *glory*, used in the sense of fame and prestige:

This obscure sportsman now enjoys great kudos, having won the championships.

laissez faire
French for *leave be*. The term is usually used to describe government policy when events are allowed to take their course:

During the eighteenth century the government had a policy of *laissez faire* for international trade.

louche
French for *ambiguous, disreputable, shifty*:

His attitude towards the affair was very louche.

memento mori
Means *reminder of death* in Latin. It was the term which described traditional death emblems:

Often you find a skull in the corner of the painting, a conventional memento mori reminding the viewer of his end.

milieu (plural: milieus or milieux)
French for *environment, setting*:

This is not the right milieu for thinking creatively.

née
French for *born*. It is used in public notices of marriages and deaths to indicate a woman's maiden name:

Mrs Sarah Cobbett (née Latham) died on Tuesday.

non compos mentis
Latin for *not in control of one's mind*:

He was so drunk, he was *non compos mentis*.

non sequitur
Latin for *it does not follow*:

The idea that you can tell what the summer weather will be by where frogs lay their spawn is a non sequitur.

nouveau riche (plural: *nouveaux riches*)
French for one who has recently acquired wealth and who usually displays it ostentatiously:

He was a *nouveau riche* who took pride in buying a new car every six months.

obiter dictum (plural: **obiter dicta**)
A Latin term used in legal language. It describes the opinion made by a judge when arguing a point or giving judgement which is without binding authority, for it is not essential to his decision. Out of a legal context it can therefore mean an incidental remark:

He intended his remark to be an obiter dictum which would not affect the decision.

pace
Latin for *with all due respect* to the opinion of someone, notwithstanding the opinion of someone:

Pace the doctor's opinion, I am determined to run the race.

parvenu
French for an *upstart*, for someone who has newly risen into wealth, power or notice:

He was a parvenu in politics, quickly becoming unpopular with other politicians and the press.

patois
French for *regional dialect* or *jargon:*

Few of us could understand the patois he deliberately used.

persona grata/persona non grata (plural: *personae (non) gratae*)
Persona grata (Latin: a person in favour) usually refers to someone who is diplomatically in favour with a foreign government. *Persona non grata* means the opposite:

The foreign minister was *persona non grata* in the country and his visit was shorter than had been arranged.

pièce de résistance
French for the principal course or item:

The *pièce de résistance* of the dinner was the salmon en croûte.

post mortem
Means *after death* in Latin. It refers to the medical examination of a corpse to discover the cause of death:

The results of the post mortem showed that he died from natural causes.

prima facie
Literally, Latin for *at first face*. In English, *on first impression:*

This seems, prima facie, the answer we are looking for.

pro rata
Means *in proportion* in Latin:

The salary will be pro rata age and experience.

pro tempore
Latin for *for the time being*. It is usually shortened to *pro tem* in conversation:

I will be responsible for the book-keeping *pro tem*.

raison d'être
French for a *reason for existence:*

His *raison d'être* seems to be exploiting people.

rapport
Means, in French, feeling a sympathy and understanding for someone else:

I felt an instant rapport with her.

savoir-faire
French for *skill, knowhow:*

She showed great savoir-faire in persuading people to do things they didn't want to do.

soi-disant
French for *self-styled:*

He was a *soi-disant* writer whose prose was incomprehensible.

status quo
Means *the state in which* in Latin, used to mean as things are or were. It is a legal term used in official language:

Now that the management have revoked their decision, the status quo has been restored.

tableau (plural: **tableaux** or **tableaus**)
French for *picture* or *sight*, used in English to mean a *living picture* – a representation of a picture by people in costume:

When the children went to the gallery they dressed up and created a tableau of one of the paintings.

tête-à-tête

Literally, in French, *head to head*. In English usage it means an intimate conversation between two people:

Come for coffee, and we'll have a tête-à-tête about it.

tour de force (plural: *tours de force*)

French for a feat of strength or a distinguished performance:

The stunts in the film really were a *tour de force*.

vice versa

Latin for *the other way round*:

If the price of apples goes down, people buy more, and vice versa.

virtuoso (plural: virtuosos or virtuosi)

Italian for an artist (originally a musician) of the highest skill:

Kathleen Ferrier was a virtuoso singer.

vis-à-vis

French for *face to face*. In its English use, it is a somewhat clumsy and pompous expression better replaced by *about*, but since you will hear and see it you should be familiar with its meaning:

What do you think vis-à-vis the new proposals?

Letter writing

Writing letters used to be the only means of communication, and people had a great deal more practice in it than they do today. One need only look at the volumes of correspondence of the great Victorians for evidence of this. The telephone has long superseded letters for personal communication and has largely taken over in business communication.

The rules of writing good letters are simple, but they require a lot of care and practice. One of the difficulties obstructing good communication is that time is often too short to consider what is being said, and how. But it is always worth taking a little trouble.

A clear and coherent letter will be immediately understandable to the correspondent, who is likely to prefer it to an inarticulate, long-winded letter. A good letter is like looking someone in the eye while speaking to them; it directly faces the subject. A poor letter is similar to those eyes which do not look at the object in front of them but wander everywhere else.

There are three main rules to remember when writing business letters:

(1) *Do not be unnecessarily formal.* You may not be writing to a friend, but there is no need to be aloof and think you are writing to an object not a person. Avoid using distancing phrases like 'It is regretted that ...' for 'I am sorry that ...'

(2) *Keep to the point and avoid verbosity.* Inform the receiver only of what he or she wishes to know – that will save everybody's time. Be careful that the redundant words and phrases discussed on pp 44–45 do not creep into your letters.

(3) *Be sincere and respectful.* It is easy to let a tone of boredom and condescension slip into some letters, especially the more tedious ones. Finding the right tone is perhaps the most difficult skill, but you will be halfway there if you sound friendly rather than aloof and if you keep to the point. Excessive formality and verbosity are both likely to alienate your correspondent.

Here is an example of an ill-written letter, long-winded, muddled and faintly patronizing. Following it is a better alternative. We'll assume that the letter comes from the Consumer Service Department of a major food retailer; 'house' styles of lay-out differ, but in this case the preference is for no punctuation after names or addresses, and for these to be ranged left together with unindented paragraphs.

> Company letterheading: name
> and address followed by the
> usual details, date and a
> reference number.

Mr John Abbott
73 Park Terrace
Brighton
Sussex

Dear Sir

I would like to thank you for your letter dated April 19th with regard to your complaint about a number of our products. It is regretted that there is any cause for customer dissatisfaction for we try and ensure that our products are of the highest possible standard. I must inform you that your letter is the first of its kind for many years and we assume that the majority of our customers are entirely satisfied with our goods. I will send the letter to the relevant department for their perusal and will reply forthwith when they have communicated to me. I hope we can reach a satisfactory conclusion when the department in question have sent me their report. I envisage that this will be within the next week to two weeks.

Yours faithfully

J. M. Jones
for Good Foods Ltd

Now for the better alternative, following on from the same heading:

Dear Mr Abbott

Thank you for your letter of April 19th. I am sorry that you have had reason to complain about our 'Spicy Pork Sausages' and 'Mildly Salted Butter' and I am sending your letter straight on to the Meat and Dairy Department for a detailed answer. We try to ensure that our products meet the highest standards and are usually confident that our customers are pleased with them, for we have not received a complaint for many years.

I shall write to you again as soon as these departments have sent me their comments, which will be within the next fortnight. I promise then to give a full answer to your letter.

Yours sincerely

Jack Jones
Consumer Service Department

This letter has been substantially changed, the main difference being that the second draft is much more specific than the first, making the writer sound more concerned and courteous. The second draft begins with *Dear Mr Abbott* and closes *Yours sincerely*; it is always better to address someone by name if you know it and the impersonal *Yours faithfully* should not then be used. Notice, too, that the writer has given his full name instead of hiding behind anonymous initials, and that he's told Mr Abbott which department he works in.

The second draft then shortens *I would like to thank you* to the simple *Thank you*. The long-winded prepositional phrase *with regard to ...* and the abstract *any cause for customer dissatisfaction* and *it is regretted* are omitted; the second version apologizes to the customer and defends the product in a much more precise and direct way. In the second draft the products are named, whereas in the first the writer has not taken the trouble to acknowledge specifically what the customer is complaining about. The second version then tells the customer to whom he is passing on his letter (again he names them specifically, unlike the first draft), rather than rebuking the customer by telling him that his letter must be a freak (*I must inform you...*). The second draft changes the assumption of general satisfaction to confidence, a less presumptuous position. The abstract *satisfactory conclusion* becomes the frank *I promise then to give a full answer;* the archaic *perusal* and *forthwith* are omitted and *communicated* becomes *have sent me their comments; I envisage that this will be within the next week to two weeks* becomes the more precise *which will be within the next fortnight.*

This letter has dealt with the subject of apology. Writing a good letter of complaint is also quite a skill. Take the following example and compare it with the second version below:

Dear Sirs,

I desire to express my irritation with respect to a recent appointment with your executive with whom we were aiming at full liaison and co-operation. It was distressing to acknowledge that he arrived a considerable time after the arranged time and because of impunctuality was incapable of being in attendance throughout the meeting. Neither did he offer the qualities and suggestions that your company had lead us to understand would assist us in this complex time. He displayed active indifference in the face of the particular difficulties about which we were at pains to enlighten him and advised us only on areas about which we are comparatively less concerned. Allow me to repeat my dissatisfaction over the treatment received by your adviser who presumably is employed by you and others to advise firms on their accounts; it can only be said that he did little more than waste our time.

Yours faithfully,

Dear Sirs,

The meeting with your executive last week has caused immense irritation. As we had employed our consultant for a specific purpose and with a specific aim, we were depending on his full co-operation and assistance. Instead we spent a wasted morning. First he was considerably late for the meeting and so missed an important part of the discussion. His advice to us and his general manner then turned out to be extremely disappointing, if not objectionable. He appeared quite unconcerned about the particular anxieties which we carefully explained to him and could give advice only on areas which are not at present a priority.

Your employee was recommended to us as a trained and experienced accounts adviser. This recommendation turned out to be false.

I look forward to your comments.

Yours faithfully,

It is not difficult to see how much more forceful and intelligible the second draft is. All the verbosities and illiterate mistakes have either been omitted or condensed, with the result that the letter succeeds in conveying the writer's feelings; in the first draft he hides behind meaningless circumlocutions.

Figures of speech

Figures of speech are expressions which add colour and emphasis to language. They are used all the time and you should be able to identify them. Many are epitomized in the writings of famous authors, as some of the following extracts will show.

Antithesis

This consists of contrasts illustrated by the choice or arrangement of words:

Marriage has many pains, but celibacy has no pleasures.   (Johnson)
To err is human, to forgive, divine.   (Pope)
The child is father of the Man.   (Wordsworth)

Alliteration

This is not a figure of speech but a device frequently found in poetry. In alliterative verse the same consonant is repeated, especially at the beginning of words:

*When to the **s**essions of **s**weet **s**ilent thought*
*I **s**ummon up remembrance of things past,*
*I **s**igh the lack of many a thing I **s**ought,*
*And **w**ith old **w**oes new **w**ail my dear times' **w**aste.*   (Shakespeare)

Colloquialism

A colloquial word, phrase or expression is one which is in everyday use in conversation and in informal writing. You shouldn't use a colloquialism when making formal speeches, writing in exams and so forth, unless you can be sure that your audience will accept it and not think it slang. Colloquialisms are not slang expressions, but there is a tendency for borderline slang to become colloquial in time – you (or those who read and hear your words) may not know where to draw the line. The following example includes a colloquialism at the end of each sentence:

I asked him why he didn't tell me that things were in a mess. If he had, I would have given him a hand.

Epigram

An epigram is a short, witty statement which is usually intended to be satiric. Epigrams used to be written in verse and prose, but they are now almost always found in prose only:

Liberty means responsibility. That is why most men dread it.   (Shaw)

In married life, three is company and two none.   (Wilde)

Euphemism

A euphemism puts a mild and deflating expression in place of a blunt and realistic one. If used properly, euphemisms can make language suitably discreet. If misused, as they frequently are, they simply disguise the truth. Here are some common euphemisms:

pass away (instead of *die*)
of a certain age (instead of *middle-aged*)
low-ability groups (instead of *slow learners*)

Hyperbole

Hyperbole uses exaggeration for emphasis, often for intended humour:

He nearly died of laughter.

*I'll put a girdle round about the earth
In forty minutes.*   (Shakespeare)

As her hands and arms were formed to give blows with great mischief to an enemy, so was her face as well contrived to receive blows without any great injury to herself: her nose being already flat to her face; her lips were so large, that no swelling could be perceived in them, and moreover they were so hard, that a fist could hardly make any impresion on them.
(Fielding)

Idiom

An idiom is not so much a figure of speech, more an expression, phrase or construction which is peculiar to a language and which generally has a different meaning to its grammatical or logical one. Although it may bend the established rules of grammar, long usage has resulted in it becoming accepted as 'correct'. For example:

They each did their best.

According to the rules of agreement (see **Grammatical bad habits**) 'each' requires singular pronouns, etc. The idiom has arisen out of mixing *They all did their best* with *Each of them did his best.*

There are thousands of idioms in English, many of which consist of words used together for emphasis (hyperbole) or understatement (litotes), and as similes or metaphors:

He couldn't have looked properly for the bag, which was as large as life upon the table. Since it contained his passport, he would have been in a spot of bother had he lost it. His mother used to hold forth about her absent-minded son, but no wonder he was so forgetful – when he was kneehigh to a grasshopper she left him on a bus and it was only by chance that he was found asleep in the garage.

Malapropism

To use malapropisms is to misuse polysyllabic words by susbstituting for the correct word one which almost sounds the same. The term is named after Mrs Malaprop, a character in Sheridan's play *The Rivals*, who was always confusing her vocabulary:

She's as headstrong as an allegory on the banks of the Nile.

Similar-sounding words (see **Words of similar form but different meaning**) often result in malapropisms, although the latter are always associated with comic literature, for example a certain character in Smollett's *Humphrey Clinker*:

... it shall never be said that I menchioned [mentioned] *a syllabub* [syllable] *of the matter ... and I pray constantly for grease* [grace].

Metaphor

Metaphors are the commonest figures of speech. A metaphor implicitly makes a comparison with something else, but also identifies the object described with the figurative meaning. For example:

The garden invited me to explore its hidden paths.

In this sentence *invited* is used metaphorically, for gardens cannot invite things literally. It conveys the attractiveness of the garden. Metaphors are part of everyday speech:

He had stolen her heart away.
The sun was beating down that day.
The whole affair was shrouded in secrecy.

Onomatopoeia

The sound of onomatopoeic words suggests their meaning: *slap, crash, pop*. Onomatopoeia in poetry can mean, more generally, the way the sound and rhythm of the words reflects the sense:

So all day long the noise of battle roll'd
Among the mountains by the winter sea.　　　(Tennyson)

The sunny slow lulling afternoon yawns and moons through the dozy town.
The sea lolls, laps and idles in, with fishes sleeping in its lap.
(Dylan Thomas)

Oxymoron

An oxymoron is closely related to the devices of antithesis and paradox, combining contradictory words for a particular effect. For example, you might say that it was *a painful pleasure* to part with your money after losing a bet with your friend tht he'd never get that marvellous job! Be careful how you use this figure of speech; the results can sometimes be ridiculous rather than clever.

Paradox

A paradox is a self-contradictory statement which contains a truth often, but not necessarily, used for humorous effect:

She had the will to fail.
His appearance was carefully untidy.

Simile

A simile is a very useful figure of speech which explicitly likens one thing to another, using the words *as* or *like,* whereas a metaphor makes an implicit comparison. Like metaphors, similes are used to clarify an image or to give it colour:

It was like a chase in a nightmare, when no one, pursuer or pursued, can move a limb.   (Homer)

How like a winter hath my absence been
From thee, the pleasure of the fleeting year!   (Shakespeare)

Some similes have become clichés:

as right as rain
as quick as lightning
as good as gold
as poor as a churchmouse
as sound as a drum
as heavy as lead
as dead as a doornail
as dry as a bone

Grammatical terms

The following list of grammatical terms contains only what is essential to a practical understanding of the grammatical structure of English. It includes terms used in other sections of this book and will be helpful when learning a new language, for reliable language courses still use grammatical terms as the quickest method of explanation.

Abstract nouns

An abstract noun is the name of a quality, action or state that conveys an idea, not a solid reality: *courage, running, health, kindness, sin, thought, ability, art, manhood.* Beware of overusing abstract nouns.

Acronym

An acronym is a word formed from the initial letters of other words: NATO (*N*orth *A*tlantic *T*reaty *O*rganization), SALT (*S*trategic *A*rms *L*imitations *T*alks). Sometimes, some acronyms are printed in small letters (Nato); others never appear in capitals (laser – *l*ight *a*mplification by *s*timulated *e*mission of *r*adiation). Some are made up of more than the initial letters (radar – *ra*dio *d*etection *a*nd *r*anging). Abbreviations such as USA and EEC are not considered acronyms for they are not pronounced as words – another test of the true acronym.

Accent

An accent stresses a particular syllable or syllables in a word. By stress we can distinguish between adjectives, nouns and verbs which are spelt alike. In these examples, stress the syllable in italics:

*con*test (noun), con*test* (verb)
*ex*tract (noun), ex*tract* (verb)
*min*ute (noun), mi*nute* (adjective)

Active voice

When the subject of a sentence is the source of action of the verb, then the verb is in the active voice:

We caught a fish.   *He said* goodbye.

In these sentences, *caught* and *said* are in the active voice, because the subjects *We* and *He* perform the action described in the verbs. (Compare **Passive** voice.)

Adjectives

An adjective is a word used with a noun or pronoun to describe or distinguish that which the noun or pronoun stands for. There are several kinds of adjectives (possessive, demonstrative, etc.) and they have many uses:

1 To qualify a noun: *red* dresses, an *angry* child.
2 To point out and distinguish: *this* house, *that* book.
3 To express number and quantity: *two* women, *many* bottles.
4 To express order: the *fifth* day.
5 To express possession: *my* cousin, *her* school.

Adverbs

In the same way that an adjective qualifies a noun, an adverb adds to the meaning of a verb, an adjective or another adverb. It can indicate:

1 Degree: *very, greatly, more, less*, etc.
2 Manner: *well, badly, how*, etc.
3 Time: *now, then, before, after*, etc.
4 Order or repetition: *firstly, secondly, once, twice, often*, etc.
5 Place: *here, there, in, out*, etc.
6 Cause: *therefore, however*, etc.

An adverb may also qualify a whole sentence, when it is called a sentence adverb: *also, although, however, merely, nevertheless, only, possibly, therefore.* Many adjectives can become sentence adverbs; for example, *fortunate* → *fortunately,* and *regrettable* → *regrettably.* Some are mistakenly converted into sentence adverbs: *hopeful* → *hopefully* (see page 18).

Agree

When a verb agrees with a noun or pronoun it is in the person denoted by the noun or pronoun. For example, in *I go* the verb is in the first person singular form so that it agrees with *I*. If the sentence read *I goes*, the verb would not agree because it is in the third person singular.

Antecedent

An antecedent is a noun or phrase to which a relative pronoun refers. In the sentence *Is this the room which is haunted?* the antecedent of *which* is *room*.

Apostrophe

The apostrophe is used to mark the omission of a letter in a word: *don't* for *do not* and *it's* for *it is*. It also marks the possessive: *John's book* (but note carefully *its* for something belonging to it, <u>not</u> *it's*). The possessive of singular nouns is formed by adding 's: *boy, boy's*. The possessive of plural nouns is formed (a) by adding an apostrophe to the noun if the plural ends in s or es: *boys, boys'; potatoes, potatoes'*; (b) by adding s to the noun, if the plural does not end in s: *men, men's*.

Apposition

Two or more nouns or noun-equivalents denoting the same person or thing are said to be in apposition to each other. For example, in *Elizabeth II, Queen of England, was born in 1926* the phrase *Queen of England* is in apposition to *Elizabeth II*.

Article

The is called the definite article and *a* and *an* are called indefinite articles. See page 78.

Auxiliary verbs

All English verbs use auxiliary verbs in some of their conjugations to express voice, tense and mood. For example, the future tense is expressed with the help of *shall* and *will* – I *shall* go; the passive is formed with *be* – I *am* prepared.

The auxiliary verbs are:
For the voice (active or passive): *be*

For the tenses: *have, be, shall, will, do*
For the moods: *may, might, should, would.*

Some of the above verbs are also used as ordinary verbs, retaining their basic meaning: (*be*) *We are tired.* (*have*) *Have a sweet.* (*do*) *Do this at once.*

Cardinal numbers

Cardinal numbers (*one, two, three*, etc.) act as adjectives when used before a noun – *one dog and two horses* – and as pronouns when used in place of a noun – *I saw sixty.*

Case

The case of a noun or pronoun expresses its relation to some other word: in the sentence *Michael's garden, Michael's* is in the possessive case, for it shows to whom the garden belongs.

Only nouns in the possessive case change their form in English, so it is not necessary to know what the other cases are.

Clause

A clause is that part of a sentence which contains a subject – which may be only implied – and a predicate. A clause may be a main or a subordinate clause; for example in the sentence *The director said that some executives were abusing their expense accounts* the main clause is *The director said that.* The second clause (*some executives* etc.) is called subordinate because it depends on the main clause.

Collective nouns

A collective noun is the name of a collection of several persons or things considered as one: *company, crowd, Parliament, herd, committee.*

Comparative

Adjectives, and some adverbs (mostly those of manner, duration, space and degree), have three levels of comparison: 1. positive – *tall, beautiful*; 2. comparative – *taller, more beautiful*. 3. superlative – *tallest, most beautiful.*

The *-er/-est* forms are almost always used with monosyllabic words, and with many two-syllable ones. The *more/most* forms are used with words of three or more syllables, and with two-syllable words stressed on the first (hopeful). Some in the latter category can be formed in either way: *clever* → *cleverer* or *more clever*, *cleverest* or *most clever*. There are numerous exceptions to the rules, and preferences which are a matter of style. There are of course straightforward irregularities such as *good* → *better*, *best*, or *bad* → *worse*, *worst*.

Conditional

A conditional clause expresses a condition or supposition, and is usually introduced by *if*, *unless*, *in case*, *as long as*, *provided that*. For example, *If she had been encouraged, she would have gone far*: note that the conditional tense (she *would* have gone) is used in the main clause of a conditional sentence, but not in the conditional clause itself.

Conjugation of verbs

To conjugate a verb is to set out all its parts in the right order in a given tense.

Conjunctions

Conjunctions join clauses together. The principal conjunctions are *after*, *although* (abbreviated as *though*), *and*, *as*, *because*, *before*, *but*, *either*, *if*, *neither*, *or*, *provided*, *seeing that*, *since*, *than*, *unless*, *until* (abbreviated as *till*), *when*, *whenever*, *where*, *whereas*, *wherever*, *whether*, *while*, *why*.

Consonants

All letters except the vowels a, e, i, o and u are consonants.

Continuous tense forms

When the verb *to be* is used with a present participle – *I am writing* – the verb is in the continuous present. There are also continuous past, perfect and future tenses: *I was writing*, *I have been writing*, *I had been writing*, *I shall have been writing*, *I will be writing*. The continuous tense forms show the progression or continuation of an action or state.

Demonstrative adjectives

Demonstrative adjectives 'point out' the noun. They are: *this, these, that, those, such, same.*

Demonstrative pronouns

This, these, that, those, such, same, when not followed by a noun, are called demonstrative pronouns: *I like that. Bring me those.*

Diphthong

A diphthong is the single sound made by two vowels when they come together and form one syllable: *au* in *laugh,* or *ea* in *lead.*

Direct object

The direct object is the primary object of the verb: *He gave a book to me.* (Compare: **Indirect object.**)

Elliptical sentences

In an elliptical sentence one or more words are omitted without confusing the meaning, because the rest of the sentence suggests this meaning clearly: *You are richer than I* (am rich). *These are the words* (that) *he used.*

Emphatic pronouns

Emphatic pronouns have the same form as reflexive pronouns and are used to emphasise a noun: *'Do it yourself, then!' he said.*

Future tense

The future tense is used to denote

1 events that will happen after the present time: *He will write.*
2 events that will be completed in the future: *He will have written.*

Although the distinction between *I shall* and *I will* is frequently overlooked in colloquial speech, there are rules which determine which should be used.

I shall and *we shall* express simple fact; *I will* and *we will* express determination, command or intention. Conversely, *you/he/she/it/they will* express simple fact, while *you/he/she/it/they shall* expresses determination etc.

Gerund

A gerund is used as a noun, but is formed from a verb. It should not be confused with the present participle, although both end in -ing. Although it is a noun, a gerund has tenses and voices, takes the same constructions as the verb from which it is formed, and may be qualified by adverbs.

Gerunds have several uses in a sentence:

1 as the subject: *Crossing the Channel does not take long.*
2 as the object: *I like listening to music.*
3 as a predicate: *Seeing is believing.*
4 with prepositions: *After looking at the pictures, he left.*
5 as adverbs, with *like* or *near*: *It was like being able to fly.*

Govern

A noun or pronoun which depends on a verb or preposition is said to be governed by the preposition: in *I walk home*, the *I* is governed by *walk* because the sentence does not make sense without this.

Hyphens

See pages 79–80.

Imperative

The imperative mood is used to command, to request, to exhort and to advise: *Come here. Please write at once. Keep going! Be confident.* The imperative is used only in the second person, singular and plural.

Impersonal verbs

Impersonal verbs can be used only in the third person and take *it* as the subject: *It is raining.* Beware of using the impersonal form with ordinary verbs; do not put *It is thought that ...* for *I/we etc. think that ...* .

Indefinite pronouns

Pronouns used without any definite reference to persons or things are called indefinite:

all, any, anybody, each, either, enough, few, it, little, many, much, neither, none, one, other, some.

When these words are followed by a noun – *few people, each man* – they act as adjectives, not pronouns, since they do not stand for a noun.

Indirect object

The indirect object describes the person or thing affected by the action of the verb, but not directly affected:

They brought us a cake. (Compare: **Direct object.**)

Infinitive

The infinitive is the base form of a verb that does not indicate tense, number or person. It is usually preceded by *to*: *She needs to leave now.*

Inflexion

An inflexion is a change in the form of the word to express some modification in the meaning. Nouns and pronouns are inflected to express number and case:

house, houses; William, William's; he, him; who, whose, whom.

Adjectives and adverbs are inflected to mark degree: *warm, warmer, warmest; badly, worse, worst.*

Verbs are inflected to show mood, tense, number and person: *I am, you are, he/she is,* etc.

Interrogative pronouns

These introduce a question. *Who* and *whom* are used for persons (*Who are you?, Whose coat is this?*), *which* can be used for persons or things when more than one is referred to (*Which of those books is yours?, Which girl typed fastest?*) and is selective, while *what* is general in meaning (*What did he say? What man would do that?*).

Intransitive verbs

An intransitive verb does not take a direct object, because the action of the verb affects only the subject: *She died yesterday.*

Many intransitive verbs can also be used transitively, i.e. take direct objects: *He runs fast* is intransitive while *We are now running two more trains on this line* is a transitive use of *to run.* (See also **Transitive verbs.**)

Irregular verbs

Irregular verbs do not form the past tense by adding a suffix, but by changing the form of the present tense: *draw – drew; hang – hung; know – knew.*

Main clause

See **Clause.**

Monosyllable

A word of one syllable is called a monosyllable: *but, man.*

Mood

The mood of a verb shows whether it is expressing fact, command, permission, wish, etc. The three moods are the indicative (expressing a direct and unconditional statement), imperative and subjunctive.

Noun

A noun is a word which denotes a person, thing or place: *women, tree, Rome, discovery, tiger.*

(See **Abstract** and **Collective nouns.**)

Object

The object of a sentence is governed by an active transitive verb: *I ate an apple. They hit him.*

Ordinal numbers

The ordinal numbers are *first, second, third,* etc.

Parenthesis

A parenthesis is an additional explanation or interpolation in a sentence which is independent of the grammar of the sentence: *'Biddy' (as she was always called) was an extraordinary girl.*

Parentheses can be introduced by brackets, commas, a dash or a double dash (see **Punctuation**).

Participles

The participle is a part of the verb which has adjectival and verbal uses. There are two participles, the present and the past. The present participle ends in -ing: *walking.* The past participle of regular verbs ends in -ed: *walked.* Do not confuse participles with gerunds.

Participles may be used
1   as adjectives: *running water; an injured foot.*
2   to introduce phrases: *I found him reading a book.*
3   to indicate tense or whether the verb is active or passive: *I am talking; I have talked; I have been talked about.*

Passive voice

The passive voice is the opposite of the **active voice.** In the active voice the subject of the sentence is the doer of the action, while in the passive voice the subject of the sentence names the person or thing that undergoes the action: *Paul hurt Peter* (active voice); *Peter was hurt by Paul* (passive voice).

The passive is formed by the verb *to be* and the past participle.

Past tense (Simple past)

The past tense expresses a past action or state: *We arrived this morning.*

(See **Continuous tense forms** and **Perfect tense.**)

Perfect tense

The perfect tense denotes a past action that has a bearing on the present: *We have now arrived.* There are four different perfect tenses, all formed with the past participle and the verb *to have*:

1 the present perfect: *I have arrived.*
2 the past perfect: *I had arrived.*
3 the future perfect: *I shall have arrived.*
4 the future or conditional past perfect: *I should have arrived.*

The infinitive also has a perfect tense: *to have arrived.* (See **Infinitive.**)

Person

The three persons of the personal pronouns indicate who is performing the action of a verb: *I* and *we* form the first person, singular and plural. *You* forms the second person, singular and plural. *He, she, it, they* form the third person, singular and plural.

Phrase

A phrase is a group of words which does not contain a subject and a predicate, and does not, therefore, make sense by itself. In a sentence, the phrase will play the part of an adjective or adverb: *A man of undaunted courage was needed on that occasion* (adjectival phrase); *The eagle soared above the clifftop* (adverbial phrase).

Phrasal verbs

Phrasal verbs consist of a verb and an adverb or preposition, or both: to *break into*, to *put up with*, to *look back at*.

Plural

When more than one person or thing is referred to, then nouns, pronouns, adjectives and verbs are plural.

Possessive

The possessive case of a noun indicates possession: *This is Jane's.* (See **Apostrophe.**)

Possessive adjectives

Possessive adjectives (*my, your, his, her, its, our, their*) indicate the possession of nouns or noun-equivalents: *My house; Your coughing is disturbing me.*

Possessive pronouns

Possessive pronouns (*mine, yours, his, hers, its, ours, theirs*) indicate possession but do not take nouns after them: *These are yours.*

Prefix

A prefix is added to the beginning of the word and changes its meaning: <u>un</u>clean, <u>co</u>exist. (Compare: **Suffix**.)

Prepositions

A noun or pronoun expresses its relation to other words by the preposition that governs it: *The sugar is <u>on</u> the shelf.* Many phrasal verbs take prepositions: *to send for, to insist on.*

The principal prepositions are:

about, above, across, against, along, amidst, around, at, before, behind, below, beneath, beside, besides, between , beyond, but, by, concerning, considering, despite, down, during, except, for, from, in, into, near, next, notwithstanding, of, off, on, outside, over, past, pending, regarding, respecting, round, save, since, through, throughout, to, touching, toward, towards, under, underneath, until (abbreviated as *till*), *unto, upon, with, within, without.*

Some of these prepositions are sometimes used as adverbs: *They were running <u>about</u>; We walked <u>past</u>.*

Present tense

The present tense is the form of the verb which denotes an action or a state which belongs to the time of speaking: *They play, she smiles.*

(See **Continuous tense forms**.)

Pronouns

Pronouns are classed as follows: **Demonstrative, Emphatic, Indefinite, Interrogative** (or Question words), **Personal, Possessive, Relative,** and **Reflexive**. (See under each heading.)

Proper names

A proper name is the name of an individual person, town, etc.: *Jonathan, Paris.*

Punctuation

See pages 84–91.

Qualification

Qualification is the attributing of a quality to a person, thing, action or state. An adjective qualifies a noun: *A brave man.* An adverb qualifies a verb: *He sings well.* An adverb may also qualify an adjective or another verb.

Reflexive pronouns

Reflexive pronouns are used with certain verbs to show that the action reflects back upon the doer; they suggest that the subject acts upon himself. They take the same form as emphatic pronouns but are not used in the same way (see **Emphatic pronouns**). Reflexive pronouns are *myself, himself, herself, itself, themselves: I am teaching myself Spanish.*

Relative pronouns

A relative pronoun (*that, which, who, whom, whose*) introduces a clause which qualifies a preceding noun or pronoun: *This is the shop which sells those shoes.*

Sentence adverb

A sentence adverb comments on or qualifies the whole sentence, not just part of it: *Fortunately, we arrived in time.*

Simple tenses

The simple present and past tenses do not take auxiliary verbs:

(simple present) *I speak;* (present continuous) *I am speaking.*
(simple past) *I spoke;* (continuous past) *I was speaking.*

(See **Continuous tense forms, Perfect tense.**)

Singular

When a noun, pronoun, adjective or verb refers to one person or thing, it is in the singular.

Split infinitive

See page 51.

Stem

The stem of a word is its basic form to which inflexions and other suffixes are added: *do, does, don't.*

Stress

The stressed syllable of a word is the one emphasized in its pronunciation: *mystery, mysterious.*

Subject

The subject of a sentence performs the action of the main verb: *Simon falls off the ladder. She is eighteen.*

Subjunctive

The subjunctive is the mood of a verb which expresses wish, command or supposition. Apart from the verb *to be*, it is identical in form to the indicative (see **Mood**), except in the third person singular, where it is the same as the indicative plural – *he do*, rather than *he does*. The subjunctive is dying a slow death, but it still has several legitimate uses:

1   in a number of fixed expressions: *So be it; God save the Queen!*
2   in conditional sentences where the hypothesis is not a fact: *If he were still alive, he would have helped us.*
3   in that- clauses after words expressing command, hope, wish or intention: *The director proposed that the firm move to better offices.*

The latter example is an American English idiom which is now established in British English (see **American English**). It would also be acceptable to use *should* or *may* with the infinitive after these verbs or, in informal contexts, simply the indicative.

Subordinate clause

See **Clause**.

Suffix

A suffix consists of one or more syllables placed at the end of a word to modify its meaning: *child – childhood, childish, childlike, childless.*

Superlative

The superlative form of an adjective or adverb expresses the highest degree of quality: *Sarah's work is better* [comparative] *than Mary's, but Sally's is the best.*

Adjectives or adverbs of less than two syllables form the superlative by adding *-est*. Longer adjectives take *the most* before them. (See **Comparative**.)

Syllable

A syllable is a vowel or group of letters pronounced as a single unit: *cre-a-tion.*

Tenses

A tense is the form of a verb which shows

1   whether the action denoted by the verb relates to its present, past or future: *I write; I wrote; I shall write.*

2   whether the action denoted by the verb is continuous: *I am writing; I was writing; I shall be writing.*

3   whether the action denoted by the verb is, was or will be completed: *I have written; I had written; I shall have written.*

(See **Continuous tense forms, Future tense, Past tense, Perfect tense, Present tense.**)

Transitive verbs

A transitive verb takes a direct object which is affected by the action: *He drank the wine.* Many transitive verbs can also be used intransitively, i.e. without a direct object: *He drank excessively.*

(See **Intransitive verbs.**)

Verb

A verb is an action done by or to a person or thing: *The sun <u>shines</u>; I <u>catch</u> the ball.*

Voice

See **Active voice** and **Passive voice.**

Vowels

The letters *a, e, i, o* and *u* are vowels. *y* and *w* are called semivowels because their sound is between a consonant and a vowel.

Exercises

The following exercises are based on sections in the book.

Bad habits
Change the misused word for a better one:
1. *Hopefully* the train will be on time.
2. Don't *aggravate* him – he's already in a bad temper.
3. *Due to* illness, he will not return to work.
4. What will the outcome be *at the end of the day?*
5. We've *got* three bedrooms in the house.
6. *Its* going to be sunny today.
7. This is a *leading question* which I regret I cannot answer.
8. I am the *mutual friend* of Paul and David.
9. He wore a *pristine* new suit.
10. This is a crisis *situation.*

Grammatical bad habits
Correct the following grammatical errors:
1. Neither of them were helpful.
2. Either you or your sister are responsible.
3. Nobody would sacrifice their free time for this.
4. The two friends embraced one another.
5. It was one of the most expensive pictures that has ever been sold.
6. We did not want to see the house; also it was too late.
7. Simon is the tallest of the two friends.
8. You cannot prevent him talking.
9. If you were her, how would you feel?
10. You and me must leave now.

Redundant words and phrases
Improve the following sentences by removing the pointless words:
1. I cannot think in terms of money.
2. It is, if you like, one of the painter's most dramatic works.
3. I basically agree with you.
4. She's a sort of mongrel, part spaniel and part retriever.
5. You don't want to be involved in being committed to this charity work.
6. The sum is in the order of three thousand pounds.
7. She arrived wearing what can only be described as a provocative dress.

8. I don't like healthy food as such.
9. This is a problem situation.
10. Broadly speaking, he doesn't think that there will be difficulties.

American English

Change the following American idioms:
1. He doubted that she would come.
2. Paul promised to contact Jonathan by phone.
3. Sarah was irritating us – like she always did.
4. They were determined not to lose out on the deal.
5. I must try out that new shampoo.
6. The clerk said that he would check up on the facts.
7. All of the students protested.
8. We must face up to the fact that change will be necessary.
9. I think you have made some meaningful comments.
10. I hope you will match up to his abilities.

Clichés

Find a different way of expressing the clichés in these sentences:
1. Yes, I'm still alive and kicking.
2. In this day and age, no one has serious values.
3. With her heart and soul she believed him.
4. No way!
5. Are you always up with the lark?
6. This folk dance is part and parcel of the traditional festival.
7. They arrived safe and sound after a difficult journey.
8. Finally the car ground to a halt.
9. He was green with envy at her success.
10. You must be quick-witted – that's the name of the game.

Split infinitives

Rewrite these sentences so as to avoid the split infinitives:
1. I would prefer you to quietly go downstairs.
2. He reminded him to urgently speak to her.
3. They failed to fully understand.
4. He used to continually refer to the subject.
5. I would like to directly confront him.
6. Do you need to quickly have treatment?
7. It was necessary to immediately leave.
8. The manager asked him to efficiently supervise the project.
9. He was not qualified to properly comment.
10. I have tried to clearly explain.

Words of similar form ...

Add the right word to the sentence:

1. Will this new law (affect, effect) you?
2. The car drew up (beside, besides) us.
3. The teacher was very (complimentary, complementary) about her results.
4. It was an (ingenious, ingenuous) plan which we all agreed to.
5. With only a fortnight to go, we had to work very (intensely, intensively).
6. The game was a (masterly, masterful) performance.
7. Do you have time to (practise, practice) the violin?
8. The (stationary, stationery) supply is running out.
9. He avoided the (torturous, tortuous) road as he was afraid of heights.
10. He tends to talk in a (turbid, turgid) manner.

Homophones

Give a homophone for each of these words:

1. course
2. mayor
3. practice
4. sauce
5. reign
6. assent
7. formerly
8. wave
9. vein
10. boy

Spelling rules

Correct the spelling of the following words:

1. recured
2. benefitted
3. fiting
4. congealled
5. repealled
6. worshiping
7. winer
8. offerred
9. unraveling
10. debitted

Difficult spellings

Correct the following mis-spellings:

1. alergic
2. chaperone
3. curtesy
4. miniture
5. immediatly
6. hungrey
7. parrelel
8. comittee
9. sutle
10. twelth

Prepositions

Add the correct prepositions to the following verbs:

1. You are acquitted ... this crime.
2. This bird's beak is adapted ... eating these insects.

3. Compared ... Angela, she is very backward.
4. Everyone confides ... their best friends.
5. He was always impatient ... unpunctuality.
6. This book was a great influence ... me.
7. They were oblivious ... our warnings.
8. Poverty forced her to part ... some valuable possessions.
9. He was never reconciled ... being the only son.
10. He was finally satisfied ... the truth.

A and *an*

Put *a* or *an* before the following nouns:

1. hiccup
2. unicorn
3. unity
4. exercise
5. heroine
6. hotel
7. young girl
8. endeavour
9. attack
10. atlas

Hyphens

Put in hyphens where appropriate:

1. They worked *part time*.
2. We must *cooperate* with him.
3. He is a *little known* artist.
4. They have always been *badly off*.
5. I must *reform* my ways.
6. The *nineteenth century* produced many great novelists.
7. This article is very *well informed*.
8. *No one* understands my problem.
9. She can tell you the story *first hand*.
10. *Any one* of those chairs will suit the room.

Abbreviations

Put full stops where necessary:

1. p 20
2. Mr and Mrs Smythe
3. St Jerome
4. USA
5. Perfect Polythenes Co Ltd
6. 3 15 p m
7. Capt Ridley
8. 1st round
9. Dr Adams
10. J A Prufrock

Foreign words and phrases
Use a foreign word instead of some of the words in these sentences:
1. He dabbled in many hobbies in an amateurish way.
2. When he became rich he started to take luxuries for granted.
3. Please send details of your education, work experience, interests, etc.
4. He had suddenly become rich and famous – and was letting the whole world know.
5. Are you in favour with the director?
6. I felt an instant understanding and sympathy with her.
7. It was an incredible performance. He is a brilliant comedian.
8. After he died a medical examination revealed that he had been on drugs.
9. With all due respect to Mr Hubert's view, I still think I am right.
10. He now leads the country, but not because he has gained this position lawfully.

Answers

Bad habits
1. We hope that/with any luck the train will be on time.
2. Don't annoy him – he's already in a bad temper.
3. Because of illness, he will not return to work.
4. What will be the (final) outcome?
5. We have three bedrooms in the house.
6. It's going to be sunny today.
7. This is a very important question which I regret I cannot answer.
8. I am the friend of both Paul and David.
9. He wore a brand-new suit.
10. This is a crisis.

Grammatical bad habits
1. Neither of them was helpful.
2. Either you or your sister is responsible.
3. Nobody would sacrifice his free time for this.
4. The two friends embraced each another.
5. It was one of the most expensive pictures that have ever been bought.
6. We did not want to see the house and it was also too late.
7. Simon is the taller of the two friends.
8. You cannot prevent his talking.
9. If you were she, how would you feel?
10. You and I must leave now.

Redundant words and phrases

1. I cannot think about money.
2. It is one of the painter's most dramatic works. (Or: You could say it is one of the painter's most dramatic works.)
3. I agree with you. (Or: I agree with you, but ...)
4. She's a mongrel, part spaniel and part retriever.
5. You don't want to be committed to this charity work.
6. The sum is (about) three thousand pounds.
7. She arrived in a provocative dress.
8. I don't like healthy food.
9. This is a problem.
10. He doesn't think that there will be any difficulties.

American English

1. He doubted whether she would come.
2. Paul promised to phone Jonathan.
3. Sarah was irritating us – as she always did.
4. They were determined not to lose the deal. (Or: They were determined not to lose any benefits in the deal.)
5. I must try that new shampoo.
6. The clerk said that he would check the facts.
7. All the students protested.
8. We must face the fact that change will be necessary.
9. I think you have made some useful comments.
10. I hope you will match his abilities.

Clichés

1. Yes, I'm still alive.
2. Today/Nowadays no one has serious values.
3. She believed in him totally.
4. This is where the bus stops!/Not a snowflake's chance in hell! etc.
5. Are you always up so (incredibly) early?
6. This folk dance is part of the traditional festival.
7. They arrived safely after a difficult journey.
8. Finally the car came to a halt.
9. He was deeply envious of her success.
10. It's called being quick-witted. That's what you must be.

Split infinitives

1. I would prefer you to go downstairs quietly.
2. He reminded him to speak to her urgently.
3. They failed to understand fully.

4. He used to refer continually to the subject.
5. I would like to confront him directly.
6. Do you need to have treatment quickly?
7. It was necessary to leave immediately.
8. The manager asked him to supervise the project efficiently.
9. He was not properly qualified to comment. (Or, if appropriate: He was not qualified to comment properly.)
10. I have tried to explain clearly.

Words of similar form ...

1. affect
2. beside
3. complimentary
4. ingenious
5. intensively
6. masterly
7. practise
8. stationery
9. tortuous
10. turgid

Homophones

1. coarse
2. mare
3. practise
4. source
5. rain/rein
6. ascent
7. formally
8. waive
9. vain/vane
10. buoy

Spelling rules

1. recurred
2. benefited
3. fitting
4. congealed
5. repealed
6. worshipping
7. winner
8. offered
9. unravelling
10. debited

Difficult spellings

1. allergic
2. chaperon
3. courtesy
4. miniature
5. immediately
6. hungry
7. parallel
8. committee
9. subtle
10. twelfth

Words taking prepositions

1. of
2. for
3. with
4. in
5. of
6. on
7. of
8. with
9. to
10. of

A and *an*

1. a hiccup
2. a unicorn
3. a unity
4. an exercise
5. a heroine
6. a hotel
7. a young girl
8. an endeavour
9. an attack
10. an atlas

Hyphens

1. part time
2. anti-vivisectionist
3. little-known
4. badly off
5. reform
6. nineteenth century
7. well-informed
8. No one
9. first-hand
10. any one

Abbreviations

1. p.20
2. Mr and Mrs Smythe
3. St Jerome
4. USA *or* U.S.A.
5. Perfect Polythenes Co. Ltd
6. 3.15 p.m.
7. Capt. Ridley
8. 1st round
9. Dr Adams
10. J. A. Prufrock

Foreign words and phrases

1. He dabbled in many hobbies like a dilettante.
2. When he became rich he started to be blasé about luxuries.
3. Please send your curriculum vitae.
4. He was a parvenu who was letting the whole world know who he was.
5. Are you the director's *persona grata*?
6. I felt an instant rapport with her.
7. It was a *tour de force*. He is a brilliant comedian.
8. A post mortem revealed that he had been on drugs.
9. *Pace* Mr Hubert's view, I still think I am right.
10. He is now the de facto leader of the country.

Thought for the day

Overused words

'I am sure', cried Catherine, 'I did not mean to say anything wrong; but it is a nice book, and why should I not call it so?' 'Very true,' said Henry, 'and this is a very nice walk; and you two are very nice young ladies. Oh! it is a very nice word indeed! it does for everything.' (Jane Austen's *Northanger Abbey*, written 1797–81)

Nice has been spoilt, like clever, by its *bonnes fortunes*; it has been too great a favourite with the ladies, who have charmed out of it all its individuality and converted it into a mere diffuser of vague and mild agreeableness. That was not how the Duke of Wellington used it when he described the battle of Waterloo as 'a damned nice thing – the nearest run thing you ever saw in your life.' Everyone who gives it its more proper senses which fill most of the space given to it in any dictionary, and avoids the one that tends to oust them all, does a real if small service to the language. (*Modern English Usage*, H. W. Fowler. 1965 edition)

The careful and the careless writer

A scrupulous writer, in every sentence that he writes, will ask himself at least four questions, thus: What am I trying to say? What words will express it? What image or idiom will make it clearer? Is this image fresh enough to have an effect? And he will probably ask himself two more: Could I put it more shortly? Have I said anything that is avoidably ugly? But you are not obliged to go to all this trouble. You can shirk it by simply throwing your mind open and letting the ready-made phrases come crowding in. They will construct your sentences for you – even think your thoughts for you, to a certain extent – and at need they will perform the important service of partially concealing your meaning even from yourself. (*Politics and the English Language*, George Orwell, 1946)

Preserving distinctions

Whether we need them or not, the distinctions [between shall and will] are dying. English is a democracy, and the great majority of English-speakers are now brought up and taught in cultures that little note, nor long remember the fuss about 'shall' and 'will'. In due course the correct use of 'shall' and 'will' will come to sound insufferably insular and pedantic; but not yet, not yet. The distinction is still available in all its majesty for those who care to use it. The rest can struggle in the dark to evolve a way of distinguishing so many delicate shades of meaning. (*The State of the Language*, Philip Howard, 1984)

Why the word 'situation' is popular

There is a particular degeneration of speech, which has flourished during the last ten or fifteen years, consisting in periphrases formed with the word *situation*. Thus a war becomes a 'war situation', two rival mobs are not fighting but 'in a conflict situation', a firm losing money has moved into a 'loss situation', partly due perhaps to having been 'involved' (a related periphrastic word) 'in strike situations'. I have little doubt that the quite pathological popularity of this periphrasis, which has wreaked havoc in political English, derives from the current popularity of the environ-mentalist theory of human behaviour: people are supposed to behave as they do because of the situations in which they find themselves, and to be the creatures, not to say the victims, of their circumstances. (*The Language of Politics*, J. Enoch Powell, 1980)

The consequences of a 'language barrier'

... almost all English-speaking Westindians speak a mixture of Creole and Standard English that is really neither one thing nor the other. In Britain this places them in a kind of linguistic no-man's-land which is symbolic of their situation in an overall sense ... Many of these [West Indian] children say that they have no trouble understanding the teacher, without realising that they are making a false assertion. The reality is that when they first set foot in a classroom at five years old, they only partially understand their teachers and this sets in motion a pattern which continues right the way through their early school careers and beyond, because they take it as the norm and no-one disabuses them. One result of this is that many grow up with the erroneous impression that competition is not important in this world. Some reach a stage where they think it is only necessary to hear the words, without bothering to grasp the real meaning. Others are conscientious and alert, but mistake their attentive listening for understanding. (*The Unequal Struggle, The Findings of a Westindian Research Investigation into Underachievement of Westindian Children in British schools*, Ashton Gibson, 1986)

The high style clashes with reality

Leonard was trying to form his style on Ruskin: he understood him to be the greatest master of English Prose. He read forward steadily, occasionally making a few notes.

'Let us consider a little each of these characters in succession, and first (for of the shafts enough has been said already), what is very peculiar to this church – its luminousness.'

Was there anything to be learnt from this fine sentence? Could he adapt it to the needs of daily life? Could he introduce it, with modifications, when he next wrote a letter to his brother, the lay-reader? For example –

'Let us consider a little each of these characters in succession, and first (for of the absence of ventilation enough has been said already), what is very peculiar to this flat – its obscurity.'

Something told him that the modifications would not do; and that something, had he known it, was the spirit of English Prose. 'My flat is dark as well as stuffy.' These were the words for him.

And the voice in the gondola rolled on, piping melodiously of Effort and Self-Sacrifice, full of high purpose, full of beauty, full even of sympathy and the love of men, yet somehow eluding all that was actual and insistent in Leonard's life. For it was the voice of one who had never been dirty or hungry, and had not guessed successfully what dirt and hunger are.

(*Howards End*, E.M. Forster, 1910)

Index

144